Robespierre

The Architect of the French Reign of Terror

(The Craftsman of the French Revolution and Republican Values)

Stefan Norris

Published By **Ryan Princeton**

Stefan Norris

Robespierre: The Architect of the French Reign of Terror (The Craftsman of the French Revolution and Republican Values)

ISBN   978-1-7775976-4-1

Legal & Disclaimer

Table Of Contents

Table of Contents

Chapter 1: Who Was Robespierre?

Imagine that you're sick of the state. Aristocrats and bureaucrats keep giving you advice on how to behave and basically, enforcing an absolute regime. Perhaps this isn't so difficult to envision after all that has happened in the past times. Imagine you are protesting. The government has devised an innovative method of killing people: the Guillotine. More effective than beheading. A person at the top decides that any person that is sceptical of rebels should have their head chopped off just like the crazy woman from Alice in Wonderland.

The legacy of Robespierre is. Robespierre was a villain. French man had no idea of limitations. He was brutal, deadly and should not be taken lightly.

One of the best famous figures from during the Reign of terror was Maximilien Francois Marie Isidore de Robertspierre who was an

French lawyer and a statesman. He advocated universal manhood as well as the elimination of the celibacy of clergy and oppression in his role as an active member of both the Constituent Assembly and the Jacobin Club. In 1791, Robespierre became an advocate for men who had no politically active voice. He advocated the unlimited access to public services like the National Guard, public workplaces and the freedom to defend themselves with arms. Robespierre was an important figure during the uprising that resulted in the removal of the French monarchy on the 10th of August 1792. He also led the gathering of the National Convention. The goal was to create one, univocal France as well as equal rights before the law as well as the removal of all authorities as well as the protection of directly democratic ideal visions of democracy.

Robespierre was appointed an assistant for the French Convention in early September

1792. He was one of the top members of the militant Paris Commune However, the Commune quickly rebuked him for attempting to create either the set of three or an absolute dictatorship. In April 1793, Robespierre promoted for the development of a sans-culotte army to carry out advanced legislation and capture any counter-revolutionary conspirators, triggering the armed revolt of May 31-- June second, 1793. Robespierre declared his intention to resign due to his health condition, but during July his name was selected to join the effective Committee of Public Security and reconfigured to form the Revolutionary Tribunal. The Committee declared itself to be as an advanced federal state in October. Robespierre failed to end the conference. People who were not strong in protecting France turned out to be his adversaries. The influence of his was used to defeat the republican Girondins to the left and left, as well as the Hebertists of the left and then the Dantonists at the middle.

Robespierre is mostly renowned as the person who signed 542 arrest warrants as an officer of the Committee of Public Security, especially during spring and summer months of 1794.

The extent of Robespierre was personally responsible for the laws of 22 Prairial remains a matter of debate. The law, which came in force during the period when the Reign of Horror, removed the underlying defenses of the few procedural defences which remained in the court's power, and resulted to an increase in the amount of executions across France. Despite the fact that Robespierre enjoyed the support of many and supporters, the bloodshed driven by politics caused by his actions was a disappointment to some. Additionally, the anticlericals as well as others thought he was having grand theories about the status he held within French civilisation because of the Deist Cult of the supreme Being that was his creation and which he increasingly was promoting.

Robespierre's obsession with a perfect republic and the obliviousness to the human sacrifices involved in creating it eventually brought the country to its knees, turning participants of the Convention as well as the French populace against him.

Nineteen Thermidor the night, Robespierre as well as his accomplices were shackled within the Paris city center, which brought the Horror to the conclusion. Robespierre was wounded on the jaw, however the question is whether this was self-inflicted or a result of the scuffle. The following days the ninety-nine victims including Robespierre was executed. The incident began the Thermidorian Reaction.

Robespierre was a controversial character through his entire life His legacy persists today.

His legacy and record remain a matter of debate with academics as well as the general public. Robespierre delivered more than 1000 speeches, as per British historian George Rude, in which the Frenchman often spoke about his philosophy and political views strongly. Some say that Robespierre was the primary ideological figure, and was the symbol of the first experience of democracy for the country that was outlined by the constantly rewritten but not was ever adopted French Constitution of 1793. Some considered him to be the symbol of the Horror and his utterances were used as motivations for people to use firearms.

Chapter 2: Early Life And Early Politics

Maximilien de Robespierre born within the prior French provincial of Artois and was a resident of the town of Arras. The tree of his family can be traced up to Vaudricourt, Pas-de-Calais, in the 15th century. One of his forefathers Robert de Robespierre, acted as a notary at Carvin during the 17th century's mid-century. Maximilien de Robespierre's maternal great-grandpa was also known as Maximilien de Robespierre, was an attorney in Arras. His father, Francois Maximilien Barthelemy de Robespierre (17321732-1777) was a lawful representative of the Conseil d'Artois who fell pregnant with Jacqueline Marguerite Carrault (1735-1735 - 1764) who was the daughter of an engineer. Maximilien is the eldest of the four kids was born just 5 months after they got married. Charlotte (1760until 1834), Henriette (1761-1780-1780) as well as Augustin (1763to 1794) were his siblings or sisters.

Madame de Robespierre gave birth to her stillborn daughter late July 1764. she passed away just 12 days later, at her age of 29. Francois de Robespierre, devastated over the death of his wife was forced to flee Arras in 1767. Two daughters were raised by maternal grandparents. His two sons were raised by aunties from their paternal side. Maximilien was enrolled in Arras college at aged 8 and being literate (intermediate college). At the request of bishop fr. Louis-Hilaire de Conzie, he was awarded a loan to the College Louis-le-Grand in the month of the month of October in 1769. Camille Desmoulins and Stanislas Freron were among his classmates. The school taught him to appreciate Cicero, Cato, and Lucius Junius Brutus' rhetoric as well as his Roman Republic. He received his first award for his rhetorical skills in 1776. He also delved into the work of Genevan thought-leader Jean-Jacques Rousseau, and was greatly influenced by his opinions, which he expressed in the book "Contrat Social." The notion of an "virtuous self," a person who is a stand-alone with only his conscience, was the source of Robespierre's curiosity. His research into classical philosophy led Robespierre to seek Roman morals, but Robespierre was particularly drawn to Rousseau's idea of a citizen-soldier. Montesquieu, Rousseau, and Mably have influenced Robespierre's notion of an innovative morality, as well as his strategy for building democratic sovereignty in direct democratic participation. Robespierre as well as Rousseau believed in as the "volonte generale," or general popular will as the basis of authenticity in politics.

Robespierre was a law student at Sorbonne for three years. The Sorbonne offered him a special benefit of 600 pounds for outstanding performance in scholastics and good behavior when he graduated the course on July 30th, 1780. Robespierre was admitted at the bar on the 15th of May, 1781. In the month of March, 1782 the

Bishop of Arras, Hilaire de Conzie appointed him one of the five justices of the criminal courts. In the early days of his protest against the death penalty, Robespierre found it tough to make a decision in capital cases, and quit shortly after. In the spring of 1783, he became involved by a case that involved an arrester for lightning in St. Omer. He had his defence made and then sent an original version for Benjamin Franklin.

He was selected as a student of the Arras Literary Academy on November 15th 1783.

The year was 1784 and in 1784, the Academy of Metz rewarded him with a gold medal for his brief piece on whether a convicted lawbreaker's family members ought to be part of his shame. This helped to establish the character of a person from writing.

The two of them, Pierre Louis de Lacretelle, an attorney from Paris and a reporter split the honor. Indignity of ineligible or natural descendants (1786) as well as the letter of prestige (jail period without trial) three years later and the sexism of women at school were the main targets of Robespierre. (Robespierre was imagining the Louise-Felicite de Keralio, in particular.) He was introduced to Martial Herman, an attorney, Lazare Carnot, a young engineer and officer, as well as Joseph Fouche, an instructor and instructor, who would all have a major role throughout his life. Before his demise, Robespierre said to have had a glimpse of Rousseau. [40]

The King Louis XVI called new elections across all provinces during the august 1788 month, and held a conference of Estates-General took place on May 1st 1789 to address the country's threatening monetary and complex difficulties. In his address in the Country of Artois, Robespierre participated in a discussion regarding what method the French provincial federal government would be selected, and argued that, if the previous method of selection by the estates of the estates in provincial areas were to be used again then the new Estates General could not be representative of the population of France. In the words of Gouverneur Morris France had a pressing problem at the end of February 1789 as a result of the need for a constitution change.

Robespierre left his mark on politics within his electoral region by delivering his 1789 notice for the Citizens of the Countryside, where he attacked the local authorities.

He was also able to use his capability to win the trust of the voters throughout the country due to this. In 1789, on April 26 1789, Robespierre was appointed to the Estates General in the form of one of the sixteen delegate from Pas-de-Calais together with Charles de Lameth and Albert de Beaumetz. As the lawmakers arrived in Versailles to attend the Versailles parliamentary session, they were greeted by the King Louis XVI and listened to Jacques Necker's three hour speech about reforms to the political and institutional system. They were told that at the Estates General in the year 1789, voting was to be conducted "by order," not "by head," for the reason that their promise of a double-depiction would prove useless. This is why Abbe Sieyes resisted King's veto and suggested to have The Third Estate meet independently and modify the name of the estate. The sixth of June was when Robespierre gave his most memorable speech, where his remarks criticized the hierarchy of the church. The 13th of June, Robespierre signed up with the other deputies to form the National Assembly, which would make up 96 percent of country. The Assembly was moved to Paris on the 9th of July. The Assembly ended up becoming an assembly of the National Constituent Assembly to dispute the constitution's new structure and the tax system.

The National Assembly suggested on Monday the 13th of July to reinstate"bourgeois militia "bourgeois militia" in Paris in order to quell the riots.

On the 14th of July, crowds needed weapons and swarmed the Bastille as well as at the Hotel des Invalides. The town's militia became known as the National Guard, which kept the most disadvantaged residents from being in danger. The chief of the militia was Marquis de La Fayette. The Assembly was able to agree on July 20 the establishment of National Guards in each commune throughout the country. [57 In the meantime, Gardes Francaises were convicted as well as given advice on choosing "new cooks." In discussing the issue and slamming Lally-Tollendal for having was a promoter for order, Robespierre was reminded of those who advocated liberty just a few days earlier, but had been denied access to the liberty movement. [60]

Following the Women's March on Versailles in October, Maillard and Louvet were the ones to back Maillard.

The first group of all-female embryonic demonstrators offered a surprisingly tolerant message. However, by their arrival at Versailles the group had been augmented by larger army and more well-trained men's groups.

When the Constituent Assembly was preoccupied on men's census suffrage Robespierre as well as a few other delegate struggled with the requirements for property to vote and hold office.

Robespierre achieved success in recording the interest of excluded groups during the months of December and January. He specifically recorded the attention of Protestants from France, Jews, servants serving, entertainers, and servants..

Based on Malcolm Scoundrel, as a common speaker in the Assembly, Robespierre uttered different arguments in favor to the Statement of the Rights of Man and Resident (1789) as well as the constitutional arrangement in the Constitution of 1791, though the majority of his remarks were not received by the majority of his colleagues.

Robespierre is believed to be an anxious, shy, and sceptical, as Robespierre was never seen without his culottes and always wore "poudre, frise, and fragrance'. Robespierre was described as by Madame de Stal as "incredibly extreme in his democratic ideas." He was cool and was a beacon of conviction, he supported even the most absurd of claims.

Chapter 3: The Paris Insurrectionary Commune

The Legal Assembly announced war on Austria on the 20th of April 1792. Robespierre stated that French citizens should get up and fully equip themselves in order to defend themselves at sea or fight injustice at home.

Robespierre responded by trying to undermine the rank and file as well as the influence of the king's government. On the 23rd of April, he called for to resign Marquis de Lafayette, the head of the Army of the Centre. As he pleaded for the health and well-being of the average soldier, Robespierre promoted for added advancements to fight the Ecole Militaire's, and the National Guard's conservative supremacy over the officers class. In the fifth edition of his book, he as well as others Jacobins encouraged the creation of an "armee revolutionnaire" in Paris that included at minimum, 23,000 or more men

The principle he adopted was of Jean-Jacques Rousseau's to preserve the Paris city, "liberty" (the revolution) and to maintain order throughout the city as well as educate members on democratic principles. The latter, as per Jean Jaures, was much more vital to him than the rights to strike.

The Assembly dissolved the Constitutional Guard on May twenty-ninth, 1792, implicating it of royalist and counter-revolutionary dispositions. Robespierre proposed the dissolution of the monarchy, and subordination to the Assembly to the General Will at the beginning of the month of June 1792. The monarchy reacted to an unfinished presentation on June 20 in which the King banned the efforts of the Assembly to quell Carnot as well as Servan's call to create an (long-term) volunteer force. [158The king [158] Petion appointed Sergent-Marceau and Panis officials administrators to entice the Sans-culottes lay down their guns by advising they were not allowed to submit a petition under arms (to be able to ask the King to invoke the constitution, accept decrees, and keep in mind that the Ministers). The Sans-culottes were not restricted to go towards the Tuileries. They were pleased to see the authorities take part in the parade.

Robespierre and Marat were worried about an army coup d'etat because French forces had been through a series of brutal beatings as well as a string of resignations in the early days of the conflict. One of them was led by Lafayette who was the head of the National Guard, who lobbied to suppress the Jacobin Club at the close of June. "General, while you announced war on me from the middle of your camp, which you had so far spared for our state's adversaries, while you knocked me as an opponent of liberty to the army, National Guard, and Country in letters released by your acquired documents, I had thought I was only challenging with a basic

... but not yet the totalitarian of France, arbitrator of the state," Robespierre declared.

The National Guard was allowed by the Assembly on July 2nd to participate in celebrations at the Celebration of Federation on July fourteenth. It avoided a regal vote of veto. On the 11th of July, the Jacobins secured an emergency vote within the insecure Assembly declaring the nation at risk and deploying every pike-wielding Parisians within the National Guard. (In between Federes was to the city to attend the 14th July celebrations which was also a success, and Petion returned.) Deportation of the entire group of Bourbons as well as the cleaning of the National Guard, the election of an Convention and as well as the "transfer of the Royal veto to the people," the expulsion of the entire group of "adversaries of the people," as well as the exclusion of those who were the most disadvantaged tax-payers were presented by Billaud Varenne in her speech at the Jacobin club on the 15th of July. It was the same sentiment that echoed those of the more radical Jacobins such as members of the Marseille Club, who wrote to the Mayor and all the inhabitants in Paris "We have talked about the prospect of organizing a column of 100,000 men to sweep our nemeses away here and at Toulon ... It is possible that Paris will need support. Please call us!" The details of the Brunswick Manifesto started to spread all over Paris within a few days. It was widely criticized for being illegal and infringing upon country sovereignty.

The Assembly approved Carnot's plans on the 1st August. Carnot ordered municipalities to let pikes go for all other people, besides people who are vagabonds or others.

The city's mayor and 47 regions were looking for the deposition of the King on the 3rd of August. The federal government was preparing to depart on the fourth of August which is why the volunteers from Marseille headed by Charles Barbaroux moved into the Cordeliers Convent at the time of evening. The fifth of August, Robespierre announced that a plot to bring the king in the direction of Chateau de Gaillon was discovered. The 7th of August, Petion proposed to Robespierre to help with the removal of the Federes in order to satisfy the city. Should Danton, Marat, or Robespierre were to attend the Jacobin club then the Council of Ministers proposed they be held in detention. In the event that the Assembly was unable to impeach the LaFayette on August 9, they summoned all the towns to the arms. There were "commissionaires" of many areas met in the city's center in the midnight (Billaud-Varenne the Chaumette area, Billaud-Varenne, Hebert, Hanriot, Fleuriot-Lescot, Pache, Bourdon). The city's federal local government was dissolved after midnight. The interim president of the Insurrectionary

Committee was Sulpice Huguenin. He was the head in the Faubourg Saint-Antoine Sans-Culottes.

30000 Federes (volunteers from the countryside) and Sans-culottes (militants of the Paris regions) took on a mighty assault at the Tuileries at dawn on Friday the 10th of August. According to Robespierre, this was an achievement on behalf of those who were "passive" (non-voting) population. The frightened Assembly had to decide whether or not to impeach the king and elect an National Convention to assume the throne. Robespierre was elected by the Commune of Paris as a representative for his home district, the "Area de Piques," the neighborhood in which he was a resident during the night on August 11th. The governing committee suggested forming the convention necessary to establish the new government of the federalists and redesign France and the country, to be elected through all males in the world. Camille

Desmoulins believes the battle is over and could be able to end the war, however Robespierre says that this could be the beginning. Robespierre expressed his displeasure with the condition of departments on the 13th of August. Danton invited him to join his Council of Justice the next day. The final edition of the 12th and 13th editions of "Le Defenseur de la Constitution," a historical account as well as a testimony to the political system it was issued by Robert de la Rue. The 16th of August, Robespierre presented a petition that was drafted by his comrades in the Paris Commune to the Legal Assembly in order to request the establishment of a temporary Revolutionary Tribunal to handle "traitors" as well as "adversaries of the people." Robespierre was appointed one of eight judges the following day, however he did not want to be the one in charge. He resisted any post which would remove him from the realm of the political arena. (President Fouquier Tinville was his name.)

The 19th of August, the Prussian army crossed the French frontier. Under Santerre the Paris armies were integrated to form the existing 48 National Guard battalions. The Assembly directed that all injured priests be removed from Paris as well as the entire country within two weeks and a week and 2 weeks, respectively. The 27th of August the funeral of victims of the devastation at the Tuileries was held on Location du Carrousel in front more than half Paris inhabitants.

Locals who were passive were then able to search for approval for weapons and supplies. The Assembly should let searchers at home "to be transferred to the guardians from"Patrie "Patrie" the weapons that sluggish or ill-disposed people might be hiding," according to Danton. The Sans-culottes region has formed a surveillance committee to conduct searches and arrests throughout Paris.

On August 28 The assembly imposed the two-day restraint. The gates of the city were closed and communication to the outside world was blocked. Thirty commissioners from each area were instructed to go through every (suspect) house for weapons and ammo, swords the carriage, and horses on the request from the Justice Minister Danton. (186) "They examined every cabinet and drawer in the capital area, played every panel, pushed every hearthstone and inspected each letter. More than 1000 "suspects" were contributed to the a great deal of political detainees already housed in the city's prisons and convents due to the inquisition." Condorcet was the one who said in 1866 that the "opponent of the people" was from all over the country and was to be found guilty according to his title, was ridiculed by both Marat as well as Robespierre. It was the Legal and the Commune and departments were at the center of a heated debate. At the end of August The Interim Interior Ministers

Roland Guadet and interim Interior Minister Roland Guadet attempted to weaken the The Commune's authority because regions had exhausted their search. Overwhelmed by the pressures The Assembly made that the Commune illegal, prompting the holding of local elections.

Chapter 4: The National Convention

The vote of the French National Convention started on September 2nd, year 1792. At the same time, Paris was preparing to defend itself. However, the city was faced with a shortage of guns for the thousands of volunteer. "We ask that anybody who refuses to serve face to face, or surrender their weapons, be penalized with death," Danton stated during the meeting, clearly talking about the (Swiss) prisoner. [195 The September Massacres began shortly following. [197 Madame Roland Danton, Charlotte Corday was and Charlotte Corday were held Marat responsible. Robespierre went to the Temple prison in order to ensure that the safety of the royal family was assured. The Assembly was able to decide the following day, based on Collot d'Herbois's request, to exclude members of the royalist party from being re-elected to the Convention. Brissot (together along with fellow Brissotins Petion as well as Condorcet) were banned from a run for president in Paris in the eyes of Robespierre. As per Charlotte Robespierre, her brother did not speak to his former friend, the Mayor Petion de Villeneuve (" Return Of Investment Petion") which was blamed for extravagant expenses by Desmoulins. Eventually, he became a supporter of Brissot. Robespierre was elected vice-president of the National Convention on September 5th however Danton along with Collot d'Herbois won more votes. "We are under the knife of Robespierre and Marat, the ones who would awaken the general public," Madame Roland wrote to a trusted friend.

Louis XVI is put to death.

The decision of the prior monarch was up for dispute when the assembly decided to declare the creation of a French Republic on the 21st of September 1792. This led to the commission was created to investigate the evidence against him. The committee's Legislation Committee checked out the legal consequences of any possible trial. The majority of Montagnards favored judgment and execution. The Girondins differed on the best way to proceed, with some advocating for a majestic inviolability, others for clemency and other groups advocating lower penalties or exile. In the 13th November of the Convention, Robespierre said that the Constitution which Louis violated, and declared that the inviolability of Louis could not be used as a defense. Saint-Just who was previously a colonel of the National Guard, had given his most famous speech in which he questioned and rebutted the sovereign's sovereignty as well as Robespierre was unable to support his words. When he discovered the surprise cache comprised of 726 papers containing Louis' private discussions with ministers and lenders on the 20th of November, public opinion quickly turned towards Louis. In his trial, he stated that it was difficult to identify files with signatures clearly by his.

Damage of the Girondists

After the execution of King Louis XIV and the subsequent consequences that was wrought by Robespierre, Danton, and the other political figures of the day grew the expense of Girondins and the Girondins, who were generally accused of having a ineffective reaction towards the Flanders Project, which they initiated. Over a thousand stores were taken from Paris towards the end of February. The Girondins were the culprits, as protesters claimed are to blame for the high prices. The Convention authorized the first however, not very successful Levee en Masse on February 24th. The insurgence of the countryside of France was seen as a reaction to efforts to recruit more soldiers. Then, in Marseille, Toulon, and Lyon in the end, the Montagnards lost the power they had.

The 10th March, 1793 in 1793, the Convention created a temporary Revolutionary Tribunal, with Fouquier-

Tinville as the district attorney of public record and as an assistant to Fleuriot Lescot. The 12th of March, Charles-Francois Dumouriez chastised authorities from the War Ministry, which employed numerous Jacobins in order to hinder. Following the Battle of Neerwinden (1793) The Jacobin leaders believed that France was at the point of an army revolt that was led by Dumouriez, and supported with the Girondins. The 18th of March, Barere suggested the formation of the Public Security Committee. Dumouriez influenced to convince the Duke of Chartres to support his proposal to dissolve the Convention to restore the French Constitution of 1791, reinstate an absolute monarchy and also release Marie-Antoinette as well as her children on March 22nd. The 25th of March, Robespierre was appointed for the Committee of General Defense, who was established to handle the military efforts. He demanded that the King's family members be removed from France and that

Marie-Antoinette would be tried. He also spoke of taking drastic methods to reinstate the Convention however he resigned the committee a couple of days after. Marat was promoting the use of more drastic methods, fighting the Girondins. After a few weeks after, he was arrested.

Robespierre declared in front of the Convention on the 3rd of April that the entire conflict was an arranged taking over by the First French Republic by Dumouriez and Brissot. The Montagne increased the tensions when it issued a circular from the Jacobin Club in Paris to all the sister Jacobin clubs throughout France soliciting petitions calling for the recallor expulsion of the Conventionand expulsion from the Convention of all deputy who had tried to avoid the lives of 'the autocrat.' This Committee of Public Security was formed on April 6 with deputies representing The Plaine and Dantonists, but none of the Girondins and Robespierrists. Robespierre was not been selected and was unhappy with the parliamentary actions and notified to the Jacobins that they had to create an army of Sans-culottes, who would protect Paris and imprison infidel MPs by blaming and calling Brissot, Isnard, Vergniaud, Guadet, and Gensonne. According to Robespierre there's only 2 sides that are the people as well as their opponents. One one is Charles Barbaroux, a Federes leader, who was popular in the South.

The increasing radicalization can be seen by the declarations of Robespierre during the month of April 1793. "I request that all the regions create an army large enough to constitute the core of the Revolutionary Army from which all departmental sans-culottes will be dragged to destroy the rebels. ..." "Force that the Federal government arm those who've been begging for arms without success over the last two years." In the spirit of treason, Robespierre got in touch with the conference in order to select to execute anyone that suggested speaking to the enemy. Marat was imprisoned following his promotion of the idea of an army tribunal as well as the cancellation of the Convention. The convention was attacked by locals in April 15th. They demanded for the Girondins be removed. The convention was in opposition to its position on the Statement of the Rights of Man and Resident of 1793. This was a French political document that appeared just before the constitutional first republican constitution until the 17th of April. In the wake of the detention of Marat on the 18th of April Commune declared a rebellion over the convention. On April 19, Robespierre voted against short article 7 on equality before the law and the convention voted on post 29 regarding the right to resist on the 22nd of April. The 24th of April 1793 Robespierre offered his own variation which included four posts regarding the rights of property. Robespierre was successful in defending the right to own property as an individual and was arguing for the progressive tax as well as global friendship. On April 27th The convention decided (on Danton's movements) to deploy another 20,000 troops to the rebellious departments. Francois Mignet forecasted that the commune would succeed in opposition to the Convention. Petion the interested members of the need for assistance.

May

According to Girondin Depute Dulaure in the early days of May, over 8,000 individuals on their way towards the Vendee were encircling the convention and warned that they would not leave until the emergency-situation gauges they looked at (a excellent salary and an optimal cost of food) were implemented.

On May 4 The convention voted to aid families of sailors and soldiers who left their homes in order to defeat the enemy.

Robespierre continued to follow following his policy of class warfare. On the 8th and 12th of May, in the Jacobin club, Robespierre declared the significance of forming an advanced army that would be subsidized by a wealth tax and would be charged with beating aristocrats and counter-revolutionaries both within the convention and during France. He proposed that public squares are used for the production of pikes and weapons. In mid-May, Marat and the Commune informally and without hesitation were in support of the idea. The Girondins had to be dispersed when they heard these remarks. Guadet demanded the closing of all political organisations in Paris on the 18th of May and an investigation of serious concern over"exactions, "exactions" and the replacement of local politicians. After a few days of the convention, the Convention agreed to pick an investigation committee comprised of 12 members and a large Girondin large. The 24th day of May The

Twelve proposed that National Guard patrols around the Convention be increased. Following their insults or promotion for an execution for those 22 Girondins, Jacques Hebert, director of Le Pere Duchesne, was detained. The Commune demanded Hebert's release within the same day. Maximin Isnard, the president of the Convention was fed up of the dictatorship of the Commune and threatened to undo the damage to Paris.

Chapter 5: Terrorizing Reign

As the cities of the province revolted against the radical rebels within Paris The French federal government had to deal with important internal conflicts. Corsica was the first to declare its independence from France and needed British aid; Pasquale Paoli by force forced the Bonapartes onto mainland France. The summer of July saw the rise of the upper classes of Vendee and Brittany as well as the rebels from the federalist movement that took place in Lyon, Le Midi, and Normandy could cause France in civil war and in conflict with all of Europe and other foreign groups.

Robespierre was elected for his position on the Committee of Public Security on the 27th of July 1793. He was switching Gasparin who was assigned as a member of his position in the Army of the Alps and Marseille. Robespierre was in an administrative post in order to join with the war effort for a second time. The situation could resemble Robespierre was an informal Prime Minister and also as an unofficial Minister, but the committee wasn't hierarchical.

The French Constitution of 1793, that included universal suffrage was ratified by the August 4th convention. In accordance with Short article 109 "all Frenchmen are soldiers," and "all will be trained in the usage of arms." The document was considered useless after when it was adopted at first due to the Convention itself who was tasked to liquify itself upon the its completion as well as due to the capability of Working Organizations of Fear. The convention elected Robespierre as its President on the 21st of August. Lazare Carnot was appointed into the Committee on the twenty-third of August and the federal interim government passed the Levee at large against republican challengers. Robespierre was particularly concerned that civil servants be moral. In order to stop the Federalist rebellion He sent his brother Augustin (and his sister Charlotte) for Marseille in France and Nice. Toulon held the honorable flag, then surrendered the fort over to the British navy towards the close of August. The importance of the station and its status in the revolution obliged the French return to Toulon.

The Sans-culottes retreated to the conference on September 4. In spite of the fact that the quantity of assignats that were that were in circulation had increased by a third over the past few months, they urged more effective strategies to counter rising rates, and use of a fear method to find the anti-revolution. On the 5th of September of that year, the Convention approved Chaumette's proposal and was also endorsed by Billaud and Danton to establish an army with a high-tech structure comprising 6,000 troops in Paris to remove conspirators as well as to enforce a new law as well as ensure that subsistence was secured. The extremists Collot d'Herbois and Billaud-Varenne were appointed for the Committee of Public Security the following day. In the following day, National Gendarmerie and Financing were transferred into the Committee of General Security, and the committee was charged in charge of eradicating crimes and fighting the counter-revolution. In order to stop the transfer of false assignats, as well as the transfer of capital, exchange and banks were shut on the 8th of September. Augustin Robespierre as well as Antoine Christophe Saliceti called young Napoleon as the interim commander of republican troops in Toulon as well as he created his "sans-culottes" battery. The Comite de Salut's authority was extended to the month of September on the 11th. Jacques Thuriot, a strong Danton advocate, quit on September 20th because of a conflict in opinions between him and Robespierre and became one of Maximilien's more openly proclaimed challengers. In the course of his tenure, the Revolutionary Tribunal was reorganized and split into four departments. Two of them were operating in tandem. The Committee carried out the best operation in September 29, particularly in the region where it was possible to access Paris. Augustin Cochin (historian) claims that the shops were gone within one week. In the first week of October The Convention was able to strike out the Vendee's "brigands" before the end of the month.

The 3rd day of October, Robespierre ended up being convinced that the convention was split in two parts that included people's allies as well as conspirators.

He defended the lives of 73 Girondins in the same way as prisoners, yet more than 20 were prosecuted. He took on Danton who was refusing to accept an office on the Comite and believed an unwavering federal government was necessary in order to defy the Comite of Salut Public's demands.

Brissot along with the Girondins were detained on the 8th, by the Convention. Robespierre demanded the dissolution of the convention, claiming that future generations would value the Girondins. Cambon responded that it was not his goal so the convention ended by a rousing crowd. After the Siege of Lyon, Couthon got in the city within the midst of civil rebellion. Its Committee of Public Security was named the best "Revolutionary Federal government" by the Convention in October, 10th (which was merged on 4 December). According to Saint-Just the administration in interim would remain innovative until it was possible to achieve peace. It was expected that the Committee of Public Security would present to the convention every eight days. Despite the fact that the Constitution was widely embraced as well as that its drafting and its ratification enhanced public sentiment towards the Montagnards Convention took the decision to put the Constitution on hold for a while until the next peace. Instead, they were able in power without a Constitution. The Committee became the War Cabinet with amazing powers over the economy of the country as well as its political system, but every law had to be approved by the convention. Furthermore, it was able to be changed anytime. Danton, who was sick for a few weeks and realized he was unable to be a good friend to Robespierre who was his political ally, decided to quit the party and relocated to Arcis-sur-Aube together with his young marriage spouse, who had been in a pity-party with the Queen ever for months since the start of her trial.

If Hebert accused Marie-Antoinette of having an affair with her child on the 12th of October, Robespierre dined with a number of his most powerful advocates, including, but not restricted to Barere, Louis de Saint-Just as well as Joachim Vilate. While Robespierre was discussing the incident, he broke his dinner plate using his fork. He then called Hebert to be an "imbecile." As per Vilate, Robespierre had 2 or three bodyguards around him during the time. Nicolas Nicholas, the printer that was next to him as a neighbour, was one. His neighbor, Nicolas was also one. Revolutionary administration was accused in a lack of action on the 25th. After the end of the month, revolutionary armed as well as people from the General Security Committee were dispatched into the provinces in order to put an end to the Jacobin resistance. Fouche as well as Collot d'Herbois put down the Lyon revolt towards the National Convention, while Jean-Baptiste Provider presided over the executions at Nantes; Tallien fed the Guillotine at Bordeaux as well as Barras and Freron were sent through Marseille as well as Toulon. Saint-Just, Le Bas and others went on to join Le Bas and Saint-Just went to the Rhine Army to watch on generals and to punish those that showed the slightest hint of fraud or lack of commitment.

Maurice Duplay, his proprietor joined"the "Tribunal Revolutionaire." Charles-Henri Sanson guillotined Brissot and 21 Girondins in just 36 minutes. on the 31st of October.

Manon Roland as well as the director of assignmentats that produced was executed on November 8th. In the early hours of November 14, Francois Chabot walked into Robespierre's house, accusing him in counter-revolutionary activities and an international conspiracy. He waved 100 thousand pounds in notecards for assignats, claiming the notes were handed to him by a group royalist plotters who wanted to buy Fabre d'Eglantine's votes along with others to sell off some shares of the French East India Company. Three days after, Chabot was apprehended, and Courtois was able to order Danton to go back to Paris promptly. Remains of Comte of Mirabeau had to be taken out of the Pantheon on the 25th of November and were replaced with the remains that of Jean-Paul Marat.

Chapter 6: Slavery And Cult

Through during the Revolution, Robespierre opposed oppression in French grounds or within French possessions (sometimes in a tense manner, but at other times loudly) He also played an integral role in its abolishment.

The Constituent Assembly gave citizenship to "all people of color born of free parents" on May 15th 1791 however the colonist whites were unable to implement it.

The Assembly, Robespierre railed against the Colonial Committee, which was managed by the plantation and servant owners from the Caribbean. The colonists' lobby claimed the handing over of blacks to their rights to the political would result in France being stripped of her possessions. "We should not sacrifice the most valuable interests of humankind, the spiritual rights of a great deal of our fellow people," Robespierre declared, and then exclaimed "Death to the groups!" Robespierre was enraged that the body "constitutionally approved serfdom in the groups," and pushed for equality of rights to everyone, regardless of shade. While Robespierre was not a proponent of the quick abolishment of slavery, his those who supported bondage of France believed he was the "savage innovator" and a rebel who was preparing to hand over French regions to England. An increasing number of slaves from St Domingue led a Haitian revolt against oppression and the rule of settler few months later.

In his address to the Convention during April 1793 on the Statement of the Rights of Man and Resident Robespierre declared a stance against the trade of servants. The group of non-culottes and people of color, headed by Chaumette submitted an application to the Convention on the 4th June, 1793. They asked for general acceptance for the group's blacks. Sixth July Marat was elected as a member of the colonist convention's Board of Directors. The constitution of 1793, which was extreme and rejected by a vote of the entire nation and was backed by Robespierre as well as the Montagnards and Robespierre, guaranteed a lifetime voting rights to French males. It also undoubtedly ended the slavery out of existence. It was the French Constitution of 1793, however it was never approved. Former servants on Saint-Domingue were expected to enjoy 'all the advantages of French citizens' starting in the summer of. The 17th of November, 1793, Robespierre mocked the deputies of the Gironde Pygmies, who rejected the idea of a French republic, calling as a bunch of smug pygmies. He also criticized the previous Governor of Saint-Domingue, Sonthonax, and Etienne Politverel over the release of servants from Hati for the purpose of promoting equipping them with equipment. 399 Robespierre attacked Edmond-Charles Genet the French minister in the newly created United States, for siding against Sonthonax He also warned members of the Committee not to rely on Whites to manage the Committee.

Conflicts over slavery within France were at their highest during the year 1794. There was a debate over whether the different groups were subject to the similar laws that were in France. The end of January saw an unassuming group of mixed race arrived in France which included slave owners along with their adversaries, and an earlier employee. In accordance with the Committee for Public Security's rules the anti-slavery participant was freed after a brief prison sentence. On February 4 of that year, the National Convention authorized a decree that prohibited bondage. It also conducted an investigation into Sonthonax's as well as Polverel's deed. Robespierre made a speech to the Convention on the same day as the decree of emancipation, stating that the virtues of horror was necessary. He also praised the French for having been the first to "call all men to equality and liberty, and their full rights as residents," declaring the serfdom of two times. He did not mention the French group. Despite the slave-holding opposition however, the Convention was able to approve the whole order. The law, however, was enacted only on Saint-Domingue, Guadeloupe, and French Guyane.

The Supreme Being's Cult

Robespierre's desire for change wasn't only restricted to political spheres. Robespierre was also a vocal critique of both the Catholic Church as well as the Pope particularly their clergy celibacy policies. The idea was to spread an enlightened spirituality across the entire nation, based on Deist principles after having slammed his head against the Cult of Reason and other apparent dechristianization practices by the political opposition within France. The 6th of May, 1794, Robespierre announced before the Convention that the Committee of Public Security had accepted the truth of God as well as the immortality of human souls to the honor of the French citizens. Therefore, on May 7, 1794, Robespierre gave a prolonged speech before the Convention about "the link of spiritual and ethical ideal visions to republican concepts, and also on country celebrations." Celebrations were held to celebration of God the supreme being as well as Truth and Justice, as well as Modesty friendship, thriftiness and Fidelity. He also celebrated Immortality, Immortality misery, as well as other moral as well as republican virtues. It is believed that the Cult of the Supreme Being was founded on the writings of Jean-Jacques Rousseau about the Savoy Pastor's beliefs in the Book IV of Emile.

The "Celebration of the Supreme Being" was held on the afternoon of June 8 (also the Christian dinner on Pentecost). Each and every detail was set according to the precise requirements which were formulated prior the celebration. The infamous and symbolic guillotine has been moved to Bastille's former site. The parade, which began from the Tuileries were specifically designed to help pregnant women and moms who breastfeed their kids. (Robespierre was asked to eat lunch at the Pavillon de Flore by Joachim Vilate, but he just ate a tiny portion).

The event also marked Robespierre's debut appearance in the public arena in the role of a well-known leader as well as the president of the convention. took just four days before been elected to.

According to witnesses, Robespierre smiled with joy at celebrations like the "Celebration of the Supreme Being." He was able to discuss the most essential things he was awed by, including natural beauty, virtue, religious convictions of a deist and difficulties with theism. He was the first person to take part in the procession of celebrations with a wig of plumes on his head, and holding fruit and flowers in his palms. "Robespierre, as normal, walked rapidly, with an inflamed air," Michelet says. The Convention went at a slow pace. "Maybe purposefully and out of perfidious respect, the leaders kept far behind him, separating him." At Saturday, the Champ de Mars, the procession was over. The Convention was raised to the top and planted the liberty tree. (The groups were started by the duo of Francois-JosephGossec. While the songs were composed by Theodore Desorgues, an unidentified poet.) Robespierre made two speeches that emphasized his conviction that there was the Supreme Being.

Doesn't He have an eternal hand engraved the rule of law and equality in the heart of man as well as the death penalty to autocrats? Aren't you He who from the very beginning, proclamed liberty, faith and justice to every period and for all tribes? The Lord didn't create rulers in order to eliminate humanity. Priests weren't created to connect us to chariots of the kings. They were created to be like arousing animal or to serve as an example of insanity and vanity. They were created to show extravagantness, avarice and pretense to the rest of humanity. He created all the world to show His power. He created human beings to aid each other, to truly be one with each other as well as to bring the joy of living by good works.

Robespierre was the head of the populace. Robespierre made his way down the mountain that was similar to Moses. He was wearing high-heeled shoes that had silver buckles in order to compensate the short height (5 3" equals 160 centimeters). Although some of his officials were thrilled to have him looking his very best, some believed that Robespierre has played a well-known character. "Look at the blackguard,"" one person told me, "it's inadequate for him to have the title of master. He is God." For the two committees, Vadier, president of the Committee of General Security, Vadier reported about a new plot that included Catherine Theot, Christophe Antoine Gerle along with 3 others on the 15th of June. Vadier suggested Robespierre could be a suitable good match for her projected images. His remarks sparked a great deal of laughs from the audience. The 26th day, Robespierre ended up being angry and demanded for the review of Theot be halted and that Fouquier Tinville be removed. Robespierre requested to remove the heads of nine people that opposed his virtue-based republic and cited the "dictatorial propensity of judging." At the moment, according to Madame de Stal, that he disappeared.

Chapter 7: Robespierre's Failure

Robespierre personally authorized the warrant for Theresa Cabarrus' arrest on the 20th of May. Robespierre has never chased after a target with such enthusiasm. Cecile Renault was arrested on May 23rd following her approach to Robespierre's house using two knives and an important change in underclothing inside her luggage. The newly cleaned sheets were intended for her execution. The woman was clad in a smock of scarlet and was killed a week later together with her family members or caregivers (and another 52). Robespierre was against bringing females, couples and children from various prisons to the same confinement centre. He cited the attempted assassination against him as an excuse to accuse the British.

The Law of 22 Prairial was promulgated on the 10th of June without a meeting in conjunction with The Committee of General

Security, increasing the conflict between two committees.

The"Great Horror" or the "Great Horror" had started in the year 1898 when the number of executions was increased to two. In the wake of their inhumane actions throughout France for the purpose of removing resistance to the modern federal government Collot d'Herbois, Fouche, and Tallien worried about their own lives. Tallien as well as Brissot, Madame Roland, Petion, Hebert, and Danton was accused in the planning (or participating in) worth banquets. Nearly all the deputy were in agreement that the circumstances was weakened.

Robespierre met with Fouche on June 11 and accused him of being the leader of the plot. Robespierre resigned between the 12th and 13th June, engulfed in anger and frustration, signing with the idea of never entering the committee ever again, as when his decision was in question. Robespierre was able to create a small army of secret agents under his direction.

As per Vilate Robespierre was the one who took his Danish beloved Dog, Impact, for a daily walk of two hours. Carnot sent a large part of the Parisian guns into the front on June 24. In the Austrian Netherlands, meantime, were nearly completely overwhelmed. Robespierre came back to Saint-Just immediately at the end of June, having discovered the political circumstances of Robespierre was deteriorating significantly. Carnot as well as Cambon suggested that the fear should be put down. Carnot called Saint-Just as well as Robespierre in the context of "ludicrous totalitarians" in early April. "In London, I'm implicated to the French soldiers as an autocrat; the exact same slanders have been repeated in Paris," Robespierre stated at the Jacobin club on the 1st of July. The 11th of July was when Robespierre raped Tallien and then exiled Fouche out of the

Jacobins. The fourteenth day of July, the Robespierre revoked Fouche. A total of fifty officers were prohibited from staying at home in order to keep from getting jailed typically at night.

To escape the heat, he seems to have travelled to Maisons-Alfort which is located 12 kilometers from Paris and then stayed in a property which was the property of his owner Francois-Pierre Deschamps.

Along with his animal, Robespierre was a walker in the meadows and along the Marne. The 3rd day of July the dog escaped from an Committee gathering, banging on the doors and shouting "Then save the nation without me!" "When it comes to me," revealed on the following morning "I have one foot in the burial place, and the other will follow in several days." Both committees held an open session on 22nd and 23rd July. In the discussions with Barere Saint-Just remarked that he was looking to make concessions regarding the General

Security Committee's lower role. Couthon announced the reason for his departure "instead of be implicated of taking part in vindictive steps" against his fellow members. He agreed that the two committees must work more closely together. It was the Committee of General Security, as per Robespierre was required to remain subordinate to the Committee of Public Security. The idea was to de-legitimize the Authority of the Committee of General Security because they served as a federal and two state governments.

The Commune issued a revised optimum on the 23rd of July, reducing the profits of workers (in the majority of cases in the equivalent of half) as well as provoking outrage in certain areas.

In Paris in Paris, the majority of the striking workers had been on strike.

Robespierre could not resist the temptation to attack the convention inside the convention. Robespierre decided to make himself clear by releasing a new report perhaps in the hope of re-election as a member of the Committee of Public Security for an additional year. Robespierre went to the meeting on July 26 in a speech lasting two hours on evil group.

He defended himself from claims of tyranny and dictatorship. He and remained vigilant of an alleged conspiracy against his Committee of Public Security, wearing the identical sky-blue jacket and nankeen pants that he wore in the declaration of Supreme Being. He said that calamity was what drove him to quit his position on the Committee of Public Security for some time and for a while, he felt the happiest of all men. He proclaimed that no one could be trusted as a best friend. He stated that he was blamed for all sorts of things in the world, and not only England and the those in the Committee of General Security, were working against his. (When Robespierre was disturbed, He accused Collot in limiting the freedom of expression.) Particularly, he was outraged over the horrific excesses he'd observed during the Fear. He declared, "I'm made to fight criminal offense, not to manage it." He addressed the moderates by informing them of their obligation to him for securing the lives of seventy-three Girondins. Robespierre in awe of his virtue, called for an age of purity. "Penalize the traitors, purge the Committee of General Security's bureau, purge the Committee itself, and subordinate it to the Committee of Public Security, purge the Committee of Public Security itself, and build a united federal government under the Convention's supreme power." Freron was in the process of removing the order allowing the committee to detain persons' agents, but his move to abolish both committees failed.

If asked to identify those he had implicated He did not. Joseph Cambon rose to the head of the throne. "A single guy incapacitates the National Convention's will." His passion for the cause shifted the debate's direction. In the end, Lecointre of Versailles spoke to the issue and recommended that the speech should be published. The movement is a call to actions for protest, conflict as well as resistance. Since the speech had to be made available to two committees, first the Convention did not print the speech. The information contained in it was crucial that it must be reviewed prior to being printed. Robespierre was stunned when his speech was handed over to very deputies he planned to pursue. The conspiracies, not Couthon's words needing to be investigated, as per Couthon.

The next night, in Jacobin Club, at night. Jacobin Club, Robespierre provided an exact address in which he declared his last testamentary and legal document.

"Who am I that they're implicating? A servant of Liberty, a living sacrifice of the Republic, both a victim and a criminal." As he was discussing the possibility of swallowing hemlock David the artist said, "I'll drink it with you!" In protest to the text's publication as well as its the publication's circulation, Collot d'Herbois and Billaud-Varenne were ejected. Billaud could escape the assault however, Collot d'Herbois fell unconscious. They made their way towards the Committee of Public Security, in which Saint-Just was working. They asked him if they could get him to work on their charges. When the session began Saint-Just said he would give the defendants with his statement.

9 of the members of both committees gathered in private and concluded that the outcome was either everything or nothing. Robespierre had to be removed within a year of being in his position. Barras stated that should Robespierre failed to take action, the entire group would end up dying. "We never ever misguided ourselves that Saint-Just, eliminated to be a more

authoritarian leader, would wind up conquering him to put himself in his place; we also knew we stood in the way of his plans and that he would have us guillotined; we had him stopped," Barere declares. (Throughout 13 months in the Convention suffered the loss of 135 delegates and 67 of them were executed. took their own lives, or went on to pass into prison.) In the meantime, indulgents and extremes have joined forces with those who oppose the man. Laurent Lecointre was the coup's birther, with Barere, Freron, Barras, Tallien, Thuriot, Courtois, Rovere, Garnier de l'Aube and Guffroy aiding the rebels. (Fouche was hiding because he had decided to not taking part anymore.) Every one of them was prepared to take participation in the attack. They decided that Hanriot and his assistants de-camp Boulanger and Lavalettethe general district attorney Dumas as well as Dumas, the Duplay family, as well as the Printer Charles-Leopold Nicolas would need to be held in the first place and left Robespierre on his own.

Saint-Just walked into the meeting at noon, determined to blame every incident to Billaud, Collot d'Herbois, and Carnot. (Robespierre was seated at the front of the court.) "I am from no side; I'll compete against them all," Robespierre declared. After some time, Tallien stopped him and began the assault, with the two motives to search at the cause of death for Robespierre. Robespierre did not release Theresa Cabarrus the night before. "A member of the federal government was left alone the other day and gave a speech in his own name; today another member of the federal government did the exact same." Lebas attempted to defend the triumvirs. However, he was snubbed, but Billaud continued. "The president of the advanced tribunal [Dumas] freely advised to the Jacobins the other day that all impure men be expelled from the Convention." Billaud-

Varennes moaned over what he'd been treated the night prior at the Jacobin club. He also complained that Saint-Just couldn't fulfill his word to give them his remarks prior to the conference. The group had made an intelligence system in the Convention agents that they wanted for ways to remove from the scene in the month of March. It's a great decision to stay clear of discussions about "justice" and "virtue." If Robespierre did not get taken prisoner, Billaud would use his dagger. Tallien requested to see Dumas, Hanriot, and Boulanger be arrested. According to Barere the committees thought about why there was an army regiment in Paris and also what was the cause of several long-term leaderships staff, individuals, and large development in the field of arms. The committees decided that bringing back the national guard's democratic firm was the right choice.

That day, more than 35 deputies, the majority from the Mountain were able to speak out against Robespierre.

The charges were being imposed were being imposed, Saint-Just kept his silence. Robespierre was able to get up on the rostrum, and begged the Plain to protect his life from the Montagnards however his voice was silenced. "Get far away from here; Condorcet used to sit here," someone yelled while Robespierre raced onto the left benches. He quickly became lost for words when Vadier made fun of him, pointing to that he had found a letter beneath the in the bed of Catherine Theot, who was in a state of illiteracy. Robespierre was pouring a slurry of oil at his tongue and choked from his own words. "The blood of Danton chokes him!" stated Garnier after he was able to see the inability of Garnier to respond. When he regained his voice Robespierre responded with the only voiced remark from the early morning. He wanted to understand what was the motive behind suspect in the killing of another man "Is it Danton that you dislike? ... a lot of cowards! Why didn't you defend him?"

Being Detained

Louis Louchet looked for Robespierre's arrest at some point and Robespierre the younger was required to take on his own fate. The entire Convention which included but not restricted to the group of three's two Members, Couthon and Saint-Just, were in agreement. Le Bas decided to be an official of Saint-Just. As Robespierre was brought down to the tribune, Le Bas screamed that the revolution was destroyed. Five of the deputies were quizzed at length by members of the Committee of General Security. After that, Hanriot was summoned to the convention. He or another person insisted that he would only be allowed to attend when surrounded by large crowds. (Dumas as well as others belonging to the Duplay family, were arrested by midday, and taken in Sainte-Pelagie Jail around 4 o'clock.) (The tale about Marie Therese de Choiseul, who was one of the last to be executed during the afternoon was not widely known.) From a horseback position, Hanriot alerted the areas in which Robespierre was likely to be killed in the morning, and 2400 National Guards were released in the center of the city. The officers of the National Guard were not sure the reason for this; it was either they were at the convention, or Paris Commune had been closed to the public. There was no explanation. The Paris Commune required the entrances to be shut (and the tocsin referred to) and also called for an emergency meeting in the various regions to speak about the dangers to the country of our fathers. With no approval from both committees, this was a violation of the Convention. Anyone who was leading in a "military" against the convention is considered to be a hooligan It was decided.

The five deputies were transported in a taxi from one to another prisons early in the night. They were taken to the Palais du Luxembourg, Couthon to "La Bourbe," and Saint-Just to the "Ecossais," according to Robespierre. Augustin Like Le Bas who was denied by the Conciergerie and was transferred out of Jail Saint-Lazare to La Force Jail. In the meantime, Paris Commune worked together with the Jacobins to organize an uprising and ask for assistance from the galleries which included, but not only "even the women who are regulars there." About eight p.m., Hanriot appeared before the Convention on the Place du Carrousel, but the police caught him. "Now came the turning-point of this journee: rather than using its benefits in weapons and men to storm the adjacent hall where the Convention was meeting," Eric Hazan notes, "the column, sans orders or leaders, went back to the Maison-Commune." With 3,000 soldiers, and their guns, the vice-president of the Tribunal, Coffinhal, continued with meet with the Committee of General Security about nine p.m. In spite of the fact that Robespierre and his comrades were in prison time, Coffinhal was capable of releasing Hanriot as well as his adjutants.

The manner in which five deputies escaped from prison was a source of dispute. The jailers, as per Le Moniteur Universel, refused to comply with the convention's decision. In the words of Courtois and Fouquier-Tinville any being in jail or released is the sole responsibility of the police administration. Nothing could be accomplished without the approval of the mayor. Robespierre younger was the first one to make it in the city's center along with 2 municipals. Robespierre the older was taken to the authority administration at Ile de la Cite at 8 p.m. through a cops administrator who was on the premises of the Luxembourg palace. Robespierre was adamant about being taken to an inmate.

The officer stayed for two hours or more for reasons of law.

The mayor sent out a group around ten p.m. to push Robespierre to sign up for in the Commune movement.

Robespierre was taken to the court.

Saint-Just was christened at 11 p.m. Then, it was after the fact that LeBas as well as Dumas were escorted to the scene. (Couthon showed up after midnight being the last person to enter the city's central area.)

Five deputy deputies (plus those who accompanied them) were declared to be criminals according to the Convention. Barras was later designated and troops (4,000 soldiers) were deported.

The armies began to go home after a day in waiting on the Commune to be inactive by wasting their time on pointless contemplation, without any resources and rules. The majority of people were passive, as per Colin Jones, with most people returning home to their families. According to Courtois the more than 400 soldiers of three factions seem to have been on the Place de Greve. Barras and Bourdon were in two columns just after 2 a.m. They were accompanied by others from the Convention. Barras was moving slowly with the intention of staying off violence with the May program. In the Hotel de Ville was then attacked by Grenadiers that discovered 51 rebels on the very first floor. Robespierre along with his comrades had fled to"the "secretariat," a smaller number of people.

The incident that occurred later is the subject of numerous reports. LeBas committed suicide by shooting himself with a gun, and later he praised Robespierre who killed himself in the mouth with the gun. Based on Barras as well as Courtois, Robespierre attempted suicide with a gun in his mouth. However, he was stopped by the

Gendarme. (This alteration in the position of his body might help to clarify that sitting in a chair Robespierre was wounded in his lower left side of his jaw, not his upper right.) In the words of Bourdon his account, his Soldier Meda shot Robespierre and, in turn, injured Couthon's adjutant's leg at a short distance. Couthon was found lying on the corner of the base of a stairwell after he fell from his gendarme's back. Augustin Robespierre threw away his footwear and leapt from the top of a huge cornice in order to protect his from being taken. Amid a tense condition in which he was "weakness and stress and anxiety," the man landed on one of the bayonets, causing one pelvic fracture as well as several important head contusions. Saint-Just was unfazed and did not say anything. Hanriot was able to flee with a staircase located on the 3rd floor, in which he may have been living in a condo or apartment in accordance with Meda. Based on the majority of sources Coffinhal toss Hanriot out of a window accusing him of being the cause of the accident. (It is one of many Barere's stories as per Ernest Hamel.) However, Hanriot fell on a small piece of glass within the yard of a small one. Hanriot was strong enough climb into a drainage which is where he was discovered and transferred to the Conciergerie twelve hours after. Coffinhal did manage to get out, was taken into custody after 7 days, completely exhausted.

Being Put to Death

Robespierre was buried in the antichamber of the Committee of General Security for throughout the night.

He lay on the floor, his shirt soaked in blood and his head resting on an ice (pine) box. The brother of the suspect and Couthon are believed to have received the nearest hospital, Hotel-Dieu de Paris, at 5 a.m. for medical attention. Barras denied the notion that Robespierre was sent to the hospital, claiming that his situation had stopped. An army doctor was called and pulled out a few of his jaw and teeth. Robespierre was taken to the cell of the Conciergerie and placed on the bed on which Danton would have slept when imprisoned.

The Revolutionary Tribunal charged Robespierre as well as the 21 "Robespierrists" (his followers or supporters, including thirteen insurrectionists from the Commune) with rebellion against the government in the afternoon of 10 thermidor (28 July, decadi, which was a day off and celebration) and condemned to execution under following the laws of 22 Prairial and only gained their identification at the time of court. Criminals, who had an average age of 34, older, were transported by three carts to the Location de la Revolution in the afternoon, for execution by the Dauphin's jailer and cobbler Antoine Simon. They were followed by the crowd who yelled curses as they walked towards the scaffold.

Chapter 8: Provincial Life

"The blood-red mist that Robespierre's last days were covered magnified his figure but obscured his facial features. Similar to the Genius in the Arabian story, he arose in a flash from a tiny place into immense force and massive size then vanished in a flash without leaving any sign of anything but fear."

-John Wilson Croker

Robespierre has been regarded as one of the more notorious historical figures and is only surpassed in the history of Marie Antoinette for the status as the most well-known French Revolutionary figure. His rise to the top of the Revolutionary Tribunal marked an intense and terrifying increase in the number of persons who were sentenced to death for crimes committed against their country's First Republic, minor infractions which were formerly punished with fines or shorter sentences or even causing a rift with the newly elected leaders. His reputation for being a ruthless murderer who had become obsessed by power, one who ended up executed for the exact reasons which he used to kill others has increased to the point that even historians have to distinguish man from legend. Who was this person who gained this power during the Revolution and then what brought the blood-sucking tyrant to his death? Did he truly represent a Revolutionary who, as Thomas Jefferson, "The tree of liberty must be refreshed from time to time with the blood of patriots and tyrants?" or did the man simply take control at an era that permitted him to indulge in his fantasies of a dictator?

On May 6, 1758, in Arras, France, Maximilien-Marie-Isidore Derobespierre, later known as Maximilien Robespierre, was born and baptized to Francois Derobespierre and Jacqueline Carraut. Francois had a career as a lawyer as was Jacqueline was the granddaughter of a local brewery. Jacqueline was pregnant for several months during the time of their wedding. This was an incident that became popular in the community and the extended circle of relatives and friends. It was so shameful that Francois' parents would not take part in the ceremony.

The father of Robespierre was always someone who did things the way he wanted to. The monastery he was assigned to had been the Tortefontaine monastery where he completed his studies however, he renounced his vows. He went to the law school in Douai. The impressive resume as well as a pedigree that was a result of an extensive, wealthy family of lawyers his own becoming a lawyer within the top provincial court known as the Council of Artois.

In general, the suffix "De" which was regularly used to add the family's name could have been reserved for nobles born. The historians think it was due to the high court which this family frequently served as well as some of their ancestral connection to the church that permitted the usage the prefix "De" or sometimes "D" permissible. His family's members were poor but they had a good reputation within the local community. They were mostly agricultural however they had risen up the social ladder a bit by the creation of a profitable, though smaller, beer brewery.

Robespierre was the first of many children. In the following four years, after wedding, Jacqueline gave birth to Charlotte, Henriette, and Augustin. They moved frequently throughout the beginning which is a bit odd when you consider that Francois enjoyed enough good name and enough money to begin his own firm in the event that he wanted to. Unfortunately both Jacqueline as well as the couple's 5th baby died of complications from labor 7 July 1764. The Robespierre's father was not present at the funeral of his wife. At the time, appearing in the public record, holding various legal positions, or taking funds from his family. Children were given to various relatives. Henriette as well as Charlotte were handed over to their father's sister and Robespierre and Augustin were given to Augustin and Robespierre - Robespierre just six in the year 1898 - stayed with their parents as well as siblings.

The scholar Peter McPhee points out that there is a temptation to speculate about the cause of this happened - as an explanation for his parents' wedding that was most likely to be due to the necessity for social status of Jacqueline's pregnancy than of any genuine relationship between them. However, the fact that they lost his mother at young a age, then passing her off to another families and probably not ever seeing his father again affected his life as well as his character. It is not possible to understand the exact circumstances as Robespierre observed the events. Robespierre did not write any personal accounts of his childhood. His younger sister, Charlotte wrote a few words about their early years and the things she had to share, though sad, portrays a caring family. The father wasn't a selfish person forced into marriage in order to satisfy his own impulsive tendency, but an admired man, who married below his level because of his love for the woman he loved, and driven to despair and lost in the loss of his wife. The brothers were close but she said that Robespierre changed from being to a "'noisy, boisterous and light-hearted little boy," into an "serious, grown up, hardworking" one. On Sundays, all the kids played together and enjoyed looking through Robespierre's collection of photographs and models as well having fun with his beloved birds (mostly the sparrows and pigeons which he rescued and fed).

The two aunts of Robespierre living together with the grandparents of his father, were well-known in the community because of their religious zeal. Robespierre was thus brought up in a strict Catholic family and social. When he was in Arras in particular, one of 25 people was a part of a religious organization that was of a certain type. It was an enormous number in the context of how the first estate (the class of society that the people in the Church and clergy belonged to) comprised less than 1 % of France's total population. Although there were a variety of church-based reforms and contemporary ideas were being propagated, Arras remained isolated from the latter, and remained a pillar of Catholic traditionalism and conservative beliefs. It definitely earned its name"the "city of a hundred steeples." This is because the Church was among the main employers of the city, employing many craftsmen, merchants, shopkeepers as well as other workers directly supporting the abbeys, monasteries, as well as churches with essential items.

Arras is also considered to be a key defense of the army. It was strategically located town that had been subject to an assault by the forces of the Spanish during the past and a massive citadel fortified inside the town to infuriate any potential intruders (and perhaps the raucous residents). The citadel housed up to 5 000 soldiers. However, they were not the only ones stationed at that location which meant that many had to live in private homes. Although Arras was once the dominant player in much part of the European market for textiles at the time of Robespierre's reign, it was more focused on agriculture and grain items. Thanks to the brewery Robespierre most of his family lived in cities, although they often moved across the city.

The people of the area were extremely educated - probably because of the influence of the Church and Robespierre was already able to read when the age of his entry into school was eight. He was into Latin class in 1766. He was a student at the college of Arras The school was operated by priests belonging to the Oratorians order (while Jesuits are frequently considered to be the school of choice in our modern minds, they were exiled from France from teaching at schools for four years prior). The student also took classes in geography, history, as well as French the language most people did not speak because of the wide variety of dialects used throughout France during the time.

Robespierre performed exceptionally well at his schooling, and when he was eleven, he was given a prize to attend the College of Louis-le-Grand in Paris. His family was thrilled to receive the scholarship, and by September 1769 Robespierre discovered himself on the journey to a completely new beginning. After his first day in the institution, he took exams which he passed, and later due to the fact that he was young, he was placed in a lower year class that he had been in. The institution itself was subject to numerous controversy and change in the past time, before being absorbed from the Oratorians and financed directly by the King himself. There were students of the noble class however, most of them came from families of professional status like the ones he was from, and many students were also getting the opportunity to be funded by their academic accomplishments. They didn't have to fret about discrimination, since they were all students with the same motivation and academic skills.

While at Louis-le-Grand, Robespierre would spend eight years doing research in Latin, French, Greek philosophical, theology, Christianity and natural sciences as well as mathematics. A classmate of his stated, "He thought of nothing but his studies, he neglected everything for his studies, his studies were like his God." One distinct aspect of his study at Louis-le-Grand was the concentration on Greek texts. The college offered the best Greek training available at the period. In the entirety of France there was a major emphasis on was Latin as well as Roman theology. The study of Roman writings would form the basis of knowledge shared to be shared by a variety of future revolutionary leaders as they were motivated by the stories of freedom in the face of patriotism, justice, and freedom that they tried to discover in the world in which they lived in the moment. The concept of education for all "whole" of the individual and in the areas of fact in addition to morality, was extremely popular in the era of. Since schools were run under the guidance of religious authorities that required strict adherence and conduct and closely followed routines for the day, were enacted all over the place. Reticence, reluctance, modesty and kindness were all instilled and required. Incredibly, friendships with close friends were not permitted, since it was believed they displayed "tacit contempt" for others in favor of a specific person. It was rare for them to leave school visitors could only be admitted under certain, limited circumstances.

The summer break was the most frequent times that he went to his home. By this time the father of Robespierre had left France completely to relocate to Munich in Germany, where he passed away within a short time. His parents passed away when he was in the school, and his aunts were getting married, and the two sisters were enrolled at various schools. So he was only able to see them for a brief time during the holiday season. Their older sister, Henriette, died at age 19. Her death struck Robespierre especially difficult. According to his sister Charlotte, "it made him sad and melancholy" and was "a much greater impact on [his] character than one would think." Robespierre wrote an eulogy poem to Henriette that extolled the beauty of her and her qualities.

When he completed the Master of Arts, he was given the option to study medical, theology or law in the university's end-of-course professional colleges. Robespierre had a firm determination to study law, and was confident regarding his capabilities. Just prior to beginning his studies in law Robespierre addressed a letter to the most renowned lawyer in France that time, to introduce himself. The letter was never recorded as any response. However, this demonstrates Robespierre's trust. Life at university was more lax. It was possible to leave whenever he wanted so long as the grounds were reopened when classes ended.

Then he began his apprenticeship in law. What office it was held, isn't known and we don't know for certain, however that it was more focused on law than the common and religious laws he was studying until that level. A few officially-issued "blights" against his character started to surface from this point on. The sanction was for his taking a reading of "blasphemous books," though we don't know the nature of these. The barrister also observed his studies, even attending different courts and important cases of the day and greatly improving the knowledge he gained through his experiences. The school was completed in just 18 months rather than the usual two years, and was a officially licensed barrister on August 1781. The school was so impressed about his efforts that it awarded him the rare benefit of a "living" scholarship for a one year. It was sufficient for the student to get a break until he could find steady work.

He graduated with a degree, a large sum of money and several academic prizes with excellent marks. Robespierre went back to Arras for a visit with Charlotte who was inadvertently helping her younger brother Augustin. The scholarship awarded to Robespierre was given to Augustin's younger brother by the school. They expected similarly excellent things from the young man.

In November of this year, Robespierre was accepted to the Council of Artois, where his father served for several years prior. The court was frequently won especially those that favored his fellow members of the Catholic Church. The result was that he was chosen by the bishop of Arras to be a judge for the Episcopal Court in March of 1782. It was an honor that many people could only be granted after many years of professional job and gave them a massive boost to his career. Robespierre was able to rise from some of the most tragic situations and finally gain a place in society, earning his respect, an impressive earnings, and the very first platform from which his voice was recognized.

Chapter 9: The Estates-General

"Those who knew the lawyer during his time in Arras were of the opinion that he was a spirited as well as meticulous and focused However, they were not all in agreement about the character of his. Many thought he was withdrawn and cold, while others found him calculating and jealous; whereas those who had known him for a long time considered him admirable and affectionate and a brilliant lawyer. and tenacity."

After eight years, Robespierre had established a prosperous career. He was 31 and was heading to Versailles to attend a general assembly to be held for the people belonging to the Third Estate. Attention to the organization that constituted French society is required.

The structures in the French administration and the society functioned under the Estate system. The estates were divided into three parts: First Estate (clergy members), Second Estate (nobility) and the third Estate (commoners as well as peasants). The king was independent of the estate system, and above all other things. Within each estate, there were other subdivisions. The clergy comprised both the more and less clergy. Higher clergy were generally thought to have "clerical nobility," individuals with noble blood that held higher positions like bishops, in the church (though there were bishops who weren't all the highest clergy as they weren't necessarily from the elite of the aristocracy). The lower clergy included monks, priests and nuns. They comprised nearly ninety percent of the First Estate. Nobles were split between the "nobility of the sword," not surprisingly, people who were knights or engaged in military affairs (or those whose family members were) as well as the "nobility of the robe," which were the more civil and justice-focused government officials.

The two most prestigious Estates accounted for only 2 percent of the total population.

The Third Estate containing literally everyone else. It included all the most petty serfs who were basically indentured servants who weren't mobile as well as peasants that were free to possess the land they grew on and their farms and even artisans, merchants as well as artists and scholars and individuals who weren't born into nobility. Third Estate members, especially the Third Estate, particularly the people who were free, had to pay a ridiculous amount of taxes when compared with other estates. Social mobility was basically inaccessible for most of French time, however in the time prior to the Revolution (particularly the Enlightenment) it became likely for individuals to get out - at least to an extent -- from their social group by working or through education.

In 1788 In 1788, The Estates of Artois met and determined that they believed that the "primary source of the people's woes is the vices of its government." Robespierre who had published some incendiary writings in opposition to The Second Estate, was hated by the elite of the region. The Estates were supposed to gather in common with smaller provincial meetings as well as in larger Estates-General representative for those representing the Third Estate were usually appointed by the wealthy and seated within their pockets. Robespierre urged representatives of the Third Estate to be elected directly, this was not well-received by the majority of. Robespierre was suddenly in the wrong place with those who had supported and aided his rise to prominence.

In the month of January 1789 The king declared that the forthcoming Estates-General gathering was going to address the issues of representation which caused problems within Robespierre's District and across the nation. Then, a few days later was announced, there was a time when the Third Estate was defanged even more. The provinces had their representative dismissed from their posts as they forfeited the power of representative. This spring year in the spring of this year, the French had to prepare an official "list of grievances" for the King. The list was referred to "cahiers," the ones of each estate show an astonishing amount of superficial similarity. Through these conversations, Robespierre put himself as a one of the people's protectors and sat down with various active guilds in order to help the draft of their own. In the end Robespierre was a target of the bishop of Arras and the governor and also the head of the council. Robespierre appeared to have become enemies of all his friends.

In April, more than a thousand persons from three estates gathered together to draw an overall cahier covering the whole region and also to determine who should be assigned to Versailles as the estates-general. The vote lasted for four days partly due to the fact that each of eight elected representatives were seated in succession. Robespierre was elected alongside two attorneys, a merchant and four farmers in the fourth day of the ballet. A large portion of the wealthy claimed that Robespierre was the only one who ruffled up people and their anger to get the votes. The peasants had been fighting openly with their higher-ups in a myriad of issues regarding land and power So even if Robespierre did try to inspire them, he didn't not need to think to do it very well.

Robespierre therefore was sent to Versailles as the official representative of the Third Estate a mere eight years later after he began his career. A lot of estate representatives wanted to have separate meetings, but those who were part who were part of the Third Estate were having none to do with it. Robespierre sent a letter to a colleague in the midst of discussions, "If the clergy and nobility [persist] in their refusal to join the body of the nation which resided in the commons, the commons would declare themselves to be the National Assembly and act accordingly." The Third Estate was extremely resentful of most of the Second and First estate members. The speech that he delivered was his first major one. at the Church, an institution that he earned a reputation through his advocacy of law. "Let the bishops renounce a luxury which is an offence to Christian humility; let them sell their coaches and horses and give them to the poor." It was the first time journalists and other politicians took note of Robespierre.

The 17th of June was the day that the angry and frustrated Third Estate declared they were officially in the position of National Assembly and represented the needs and interests of all citizens. On the following day they found themselves escorted out of their chambers for meeting and moved to an indoor tennis court, where they took their Tennis Court Oath to stand in unison with one another. The king reacted by mandating the estates to gather at a common location, in accordance with the wishes of it was the Third Estate wished, but additionally, he began to increase the number of soldiers in Paris as well as other regions.

In the immediate aftermath of this 14th July that the famous attack on the Bastille occurred. A large number of Parisians took over the fort, around one hundred killed by the troops of the governor which was executed by having his head fitted upon a pike at the conclusion of the uprising. The people began calling what was happening in Paris and across France an act of revolution. Robespierre was awed by the protesting citizens by writing that the execution of the Governor (and later his mayor from Paris) in the midst of the revolutions was the "punishment" for firing on the populace and pursuing their interests. The first impression is that death was an appropriate punishment in the mind of Robespierre to punish the crime of opposing the interests of all people.

At this time, Robespierre was not the person who was determined to separate the head of the King from his body. His acquiescence to demands of the Assembly and the brutal responses of the majority of people who supported the National Assembly left him confident that it was the Assembly which was the true powerhouse within France. The king's welcome was met with cheers and acclaim by the citizens of Paris just a few days following the destruction of the Bastille He was certain that the French backed Louis XVI, and as this, did the Assembly. However, it was the nobles as well as other elites who were rewarded with the label as "unpatriotic."

Chapter 10: Revolution

"What is going on in the riots in Paris? All freedoms, some blood spilled, and a couple of heads cut off, sure however, they were heads of the guilty people...It is due to the riots that our nation owes its freedom."

-Robespierre

The elite began to leave France when violence grew. Numerous mob and murders ensued, and the violence was divisive within the National Assembly and other bodies. Discussions about militia formation started, and as they were hesitant, Robespierre declared that the actions so far were to benefit a noble purpose. The Governor of Paris was killed shortly afterward due to the crisis of hunger and bread shortage that has been a constant across the city. Nobles were executed after they fled and others were snatched from their own homes.

Historical scholar Peter McPhee argues that Robespierre wasn't a casual murderer despite the fact that he was a renowned killer. Robespierre was not a fan of the violence but saw that it was the normal response of those who believed that they were wronged too long. He believed that it was the duty for the National Assembly to institute a justice system that could satisfy the need to redress those who suffered while also removing the demand for a rogue mob justice. The idea was not unique to the same thinking; other people also thought that individuals were in fact paying through their own lives the death they had caused through poor management of resources, greed as well as ignoring their obligations towards the public.

Nobles have continued to make concessions. They did agree to abolish the feudal system. But they insist on keeping the harvest and property rights in place, meaning that they had to make heavy payments to the nobles. It would cause tension within the Assembly as well as on the streets.

On the 27th of August in 1897 on the 27th of August, the National Assembly produced the famous Declaration of the Rights of Man and the Citizen. The Declaration was not a formal document as the U.S. Declaration of Independence or the Constitution it was it was a declaration of the morals and ideals which the Revolution was attributed to (or said it was). It was to become the guiding document used in the creation of later constitutions. Robespierre's role in the Declaration was smaller than the influence he had in subsequent aspects although he had input suggestions on tax policy reforms as well as emphasized the significance of the freedom of speech, media, and the religion and believed it was necessary to ensure that the people elected to office were held to a certain degree of responsibility.

If you consider that he might ultimately be the head of the Tribunal that would sentence people according to the content they wrote or opinions they propagated and his focus on freedom of expression and the press is intriguing. He seems to believe that eventually it would be an unalienable right (like rights to life) that was not considered as part of an "interests of the Nation." The opinions of him during this period, as all times and always, were polarized. His accent from the provinces was ridiculed in the Assembly However, his pragmatism did not stop him from ever making appearances on the podium. There were those who thought that he was exuberant above the norm and a peacock that only spoke words with without substance. Others believed that he was a symbol of patriotism and the ideals of revolution. He has always been either or both.

The 5th October, which was the date that the Women's March on Versailles took place and the Women's March on Versailles took place, when Robespierre made his first public contribution. When a large number of women stormed at the Assembly, Robespierre agreed to listen to their concerns concerning the food shortage in Paris and made demands together with the rest council, that the King be returned to Paris together with them. He was then which was followed by the Assembly.

In Paris and with a few inflated theories about the effectiveness in their first few actions as well as naive expectations of the coming years The Assembly embarked on their most ambitious plan yet to completely transform France according to their new rules. Nearly every aspect of the monarchical, feudal Catholic and monarchical system was to be eliminated starting from the Estates system all the way to the manner in the way districts were split. It was to become an New France where men where equally treated regardless of their place or position. There would be many years of deliberations, resolutions thoughts, and inability to determine the most efficient This was the time that the partisan divide in the Assembly really began to be apparent.

"How was the common man to be represented?" was possibly the largest problem that came up at the time. A lot of people wanted a monarchy that was constitutional that included the Assembly serving as a parliament and the king having limited veto power. Some, such as Robespierre but were fascinated by the ideals from the Roman republics that they were educated upon. Although many were of the opinion that those who frequently contribute financially to the state by way of tax payment or any other method, ought to have the right in voting, Robespierre and many provincial supporters of his wished for everyone every single person, regardless of their income (though so long as they were men) to participate in the democratic process. It was surprising to note that he was at that time, extremely supportive of Jewish equal rights.

Chapter 11: Reform

"France can be divided into two groups of the populace and the Aristocracy. This latter group is dying however its lengthy, prolonged death-curses do not go free of convulsions."

-Robespierre

The process of reforming was arduous and long-lasting which was marked with violent incidents against the people of the elite or who believed they were those who were deemed to be enemies of the world. When the question of how to stop these uprisings violently was discussed, Robespierre argued that all needed to be done was continue the reform process and recognize that some people might die or buildings may go up in flames however, the people it occurred to were not "hostile to the Revolution."

The Assembly discussed hunting rights, common-land ownership and division, which were the last remains of feudalism (which angered the peasants, whom they had heard that feudalism had been wiped out by). Many times, when the Assembly was able to only partially take away a statute or an old custom, people behaved like it was removed completely and hunted without restriction or split old manor lands between them.

In the course of this, Robespierre was not always effective in his speeches and communicating with fellow delegate. Contrary to other revolutionary leaders He did not have all day in literary salons arguing about and discussing the topics relevant to the moment. The man was educated but in academia only. He also had plenty he learned in this period as a type of trial-by-fire. He learned how you had to prove a fact quickly, or else risk being interrupted and then dismissed. He was placed, along with other people, with those who were the most extreme Assembly members. However, he did not get a chance to sit part of any of the committees who actually finished each of the projects that the Assembly were working on.

Different groups, Masonic Lodges, and others began to gather during this period to organise and advocate for different revolutionary issues. Robespierre began to be extremely active within one of them, the Society of Friends of the Constitution, also known as known as the Jacobin Club. Beginning in late 1789, Robespierre began practicing debates or talks here before taking them to the Assembly. The Assembly was an elite membership that charged fees. This was much more suited to him than the constant political machinations of the Assembly or the less formal and a variety of coffeehouse options within the city. The following year, in March He was elected President and became the person responsible for coordinating with all the branches of the Society throughout France.

The 19th June 1790 The Assembly was formally rid of titles inherited from the past, a emblem of nobleness. Robespierre made the choice at this point to eliminate his "De" prefix from his name. Although it wasn't actually the result of an inheritance noble, for him the decision was an appropriate symbolic choice due to the meaning of the title.

The main issues that faced the Assembly were the financial issues. The monarchy was robbed of its power, but become completely insolvent prior to the assembly's re-taking and now they were forced to bear the cost. A majority of people were also protesting about the difficulties and injustices that had afflicted them in the past in refusing to pay taxes. A few strategies, which were more successful over others were embraced by the newly elected government. Church property was auctioned off, paper currency was created (which rapidly suffered from a severe inflation) In 1791, new tax laws were enacted.

Around this time at which the Revolution was beginning to lose support from the beginning. Over the course of a few years it was believed that the Revolution was portrayed as a revolutionary change to the existing system of government - an attempt to unite the King, Church and the people, resulting in the creation of a more prosperous France that was inclusive for everyone. The Church was beginning to get increasingly annoyed when their property was sold to the clergy as they became part of the state and received increased pay increases However, the most devastating impact of all occurred on the 12th of July 1790 in which the Assembly made a decision that bishops and priests should become elected as others civil officials. For the Church's leaders and other those who were members of the Church this represented a spit in the direction of God and the Holy Spirit, who they believed blessed those who took the religious orders and handed out appointments to the clergy through the higher levels.

Robespierre was, as of this moment was not as critical of the Catholic Church as some of his peers. He recognized that religious leaders were able to perform an important public service for the public, but they were not a favorite among clergy who retreated from the public sphere and remained with the chapels. He was completely against the Church becoming self-governing by appointing its own leader or funding itself out from the structures of the government.

In this moment, the newspaper's editorials became more critical regarding Robespierre and the Revolution as well as Robespierre. The man had had to face a accusations of slander and was angry about the issue - and now they were slamming the circumstances of his birth by publishing the love poems that he wrote when he was a child in the newspaper articles, and accused him of not being grateful towards the Church which has "raised him" by funding the cost of his education. Prior to this it was his habit to take the side of his fellow citizens and stood up for the principles which he was most passionate about as well as the elements of the Revolution that he believed were most significant regardless of interruptions, insults as well as other critics. He began to resign. The interactions with his peers became less tense. He was spending more and more time inside his home in which he got incredible amounts of mail especially from admirers of females.

Then, slowly, he started to return to the scene, becoming more and more frustrated by what he believed to be people who appeared to be nobles or Patriots and seeking to advance their own agendas. The rumors of conspiracy abound and the secret elite blamed for the stagnation of action from the Assembly. Robespierre believed that the most effective answer to this was to stand firm against compromise even when the purpose was to maintain peace and order in the daily life. He opposed slavery and believed that the Assembly should ban it from every one of the French colonies too. In response to colonies' argument that their case that the Assembly could not be allowed to create rules that would apply for them, Robespierre replied, "Death to the colonies if the colonists want, through threats, to force us to legislate as best suits them!"

Concerning the issue of women Robespierre wasn't a true feminist. He was a proponent of the right to women be admitted to universities, but his does not apply to the right of suffrage, or any other rights. The only reform which was favored by the female population was that of equalizing the inheritance rights of women. This is partly due to the fact his belief was that the entire property after death ought to be given by the government and divided equally this was an extremely unpopular idea.

Despite the constant criticism the press brought him and violent anti-Revolutionary publications He remained a staunch fan of freedom of speech as well as the press. In 1791, he called against the abolishment of death penalties, which was a logical move in light of later decisions. Though his proposal was unsuccessful however, it contributed to an increase in the quantity of offenses that were punishable by the death penalty. The guillotine was officially utilized as a method for execution. The guillotine was thought to be safer than hanging should it become required.

Chapter 12: A New France

"The People are so convinced of Robespierre's virtue, so predisposed in his favor, that they could watch him picking their neighbor's pocket without believing it"

-Deputy of France

The 11th June, 1791 Robespierre received a vote - with a large majority to be the public prosecutor of the Criminal Court of Paris. This election increased the anger of his critics in the media. He was accused of mingling with nightclub girls and engaging in sexual machismo and living in an unsavory social groups. The man was removed from the Court in the wake of the election. Within a week the King fled Paris because of his anger over the most recent reforms to the Church. It was Louis XVI's most costly error. The radicals who feared the elite conspiracy and feared elite conspiracy, this was the only evidence they needed. They were convinced that the displaced nobles were now trying to help in the cause of an invasion into France.

Louis was seized and was released, and returned to the throne until the Assembly was deciding what to do. Robespierre stood in complete support in the deposing of King Louis, saying anyone who clung belief that the King possessed an inherited divine or irrevocable title were faking it by relying on fanciful stories. The king was also concerned that certain factions within the Assembly had become more powerful and were moving dangerously near to establishing new hierarchy while working to eliminate the previous. The Assembly officially dissolved Louis within a short time, and claimed that it was just temporary. Protests immediately began where people demanded King's resignation - but they were not armed and over fifty people were murdered in the National Guard. Robespierre as well as other elements of the democratic system protested, and they issued a number of harsh speeches and documents.

Jacobin Club Jacobin Club was raided shortly afterwards by National Guardsmen, and a few members were confined to semi-protected hiding in new homes. Robespierre's radical group comprised just thirty people in the entire Assembly He was also the position of their chief spokesperson. The man was referred to as the person who was able remain true to the fundamentals in the Declaration of the Rights of Man when confronted by people who would compromise the rights of their citizens to achieve peace, or for their own gain.

There was a growing concern among the public. Although, like everyone else, people had different opinions on his opinions There was a distinct segment of people who hated the man. He was adamantly opposed to him compromising on his beliefs and appeared to have an enthralling effect on many people, especially those of people who were deprived of French despite his reputation for rambling and boring speech. One Assembly Member said that if he carried all of his ideas and kept on gaining authority, the process would result in "blood-soaked catastrophe."

The Assembly was scheduled to come to an end, with its task coming to an end. The King would not abdicate, but formally consent to a constitution monarchy arrangement and a new legislature which would sit beneath and alongside him. On September 14 The Assembly was officially disbanded, and Robespierre as well as other radical members received a rousing reception from the public for being"the "Incorruptible!."

A brief trip back to Arras as well as the surrounding area brought him to the forefront of current issues being played out in the public. Similar to all over the world the country, he was received with a round of applause from the people however, he was also met with discontent and criticism from the upper classes. They refused to pay tax they felt weren't rightfully being taken, and issues regarding the ownership of nobility-owned land weren't yet resolved or even implemented. The clergy were still angry about their situation and particularly those who were at the top (many lower clergy were given increase in pay as a result of the latest changes). The general public largely remain optimistic about the direction of the Union, it was becoming apparent that people of the landed wealthy were moving abroad or were are preparing to move. As time passed it was feared about the possibility of war between Austria or Prussia as well. With most of National Guard and other military located in the provinces that were closest to the Council, the nation was utterly unprepared in the event that war occurred to occur.

Robespierre made a decision decide. He had to choose between the Legislative Assembly, taking up the duties of the Assembly as well as the administration of the nation, had been chosen. It would be understood by everyone and embraced his decision if he had left the public sphere. The man certainly deserves some time off; several of his written works from the last period of his tenure working for the National Assembly detail the severe loss of health that he been suffering from stress and excessive work. But, he decided to come back to Paris after his stay within the country. The precise reason remains unclear. Peter McPhee speculates that there could not have been sufficient jobs available in the area for him to make a home. Whatever reason, during the fall of 1791, McPhee returned to Paris. This move would transform his life and the direction of Parisian time and history for ever.

He reconnected with his former club, the Jacobin Club and found warm welcoming receptions from the club's members as well as the general members of the public. In the two months he was absent there was a lot of change in Paris. A lot of people were dissatisfied about the last decision taken regarding how to manage the influence of the monarchy against the populace, and a lot of Parisians remain angry with Louis XVI for his failed attempts to flee his city. Numerous army officers who were part of the elite left with the nobles. As December came around, they'd dropped 6000.

To counter the devastating reduction in wealthy people as well as military officers with training The Legislative Assembly passed a law to ensure that any person who emigrated didn't return before 1792's end was considered to be an infraction, guilty of conspiracy and sentenced to death. Louis could suspend the law before it took the law (his power made it difficult to completely block a law and he had the power to hold off the implementation of a law to give an opportunity for opposition party members to gather support and vote the bill down). Nobles were more secure for the moment however the fact it was able to make it onto the office of Louis XVI is a good illustration of how popular views were on the nobles.

Since he wasn't an elected member of the Legislative Assembly, Robespierre had to employ the tactics of many other educated, passionate patriots, which included writings and scheduled gatherings. When it was the Legislative Assembly was deciding whether or whether to declare battle, since Louis Jacobins' brothers had put together the court of enemies during their exile. Robespierre as well as Jacobins Jacobins attempted to convince the entire assembly by delivering speeches and writings that it was utter mistake to engage in outside of the country when there was still a lot to be solved in the nation. Instead, the focus should be in promoting the arts and other aspects of the culture of France and making the army ready only for defense.

The opposition was not as strong for his efforts to stop war, because the majority of Revolutionaries were still convinced that the entire the nobles who fled - including certain people within the country are part of an enormous plot to undermine the newly established France by attacking foreign allies. The only ones he had were his trusted friends who stood close to him and made a statement in his defense. In the month of February 1792, the official swearing ceremony was completed. into the post of prosecutor public and was able to split his time between his new position as well as Revolutionary actions. In April, to his displeasure his displeasure, war on Austria was officially declared. His name took the most severe blow to his reputation thus far and even ordinary people who always adored him, feeling that his views on war were against France.

Noblemen and mayors continued to be killed. Robespierre was, again was not in support of the infringement of law of the masses, however he claimed it was a normal consequence of the crimes against the people these wealthy people were responsible for. Robespierre was extremely skeptical of the military's top brass who were unable to distinguish them in his opinion as opposed to the leaders of the military previously who committed to firing upon demonstrators. Though this wasn't often the case however, his admonitions about the dangers of war were proving to be accurate. France did not do good. The country was losing fights repeatedly in increasing people were in favor of the creation of a republic. created.

Robespierre did not support. He was a fan of the republican system however was skeptical about its ability to be able to function on a massive number of people and thought a larger educated and well-educated populace was necessary for it to succeed (hence his previous assertion on the need for culture and education to be developed). He stated that, in fact legally, a republican. However "I would rather see a popular representative assembly and free and respected citizens with a king than a People enslaved and degraded under the whip of an aristocratic senate and dictator." He believed the idea of a democratic legislature in the wake of deposing the king might be a viable option between a real republic and real monarchy. In the end, however, the Prussian army was fighting in the defence of the monarchy However, make it clear that they'd respond with a retaliation if harm occurred to the monarchy or family members of the monarch.

Chapter 13: Tribunal

"The Brissotins' [Robespierre's revolutionary adversaries'] success in their campaign to start a military campaign for national defense made the nation vulnerable to invasion and increased the expectations of everyone who opposed the Revolution. The campaign also exposed themto accusations that they had a shady relationship with...the monarch, with an effort to prevent from allowing power to fall to the hands of Parisian radicals, which included Robespierre. The establishment of the Revolutionary Tribunal in a context of bloodletting, recrimination and uncertainty rendered unaffordable any hope for a reconciliation with the old allies."

-Peter McPhee

On the 15th of August 1792 Robespierre declared to the Commune as well as the Assembly the need to establish an Revolutionary Tribunal with jurors who were selected out of "each section, sovereign and without further appeal." It was believed that the present courts had too narrow an emphasis, concept and distorted views when handling revolutionary protests and other crimes that were committed under the name of the populace. The need was for one that was aware of the particular circumstances that surrounded what the citizens needed.

The opposition groups that had spoken about Robespierre was, as a result of the numerous military mistakes, currently at their lowest. Robespierre began to become more devoted to his personal causes and certain long-standing friendships began suffering because of this. Many felt that the creation of the tribunal was sufficient to disintegrate old relations. After he learned that the people who were involved in the uprising that caused the deaths of a number of guards were facing the death penalty He sought to have two of the most prominent prosecutors detained. His enemies launched a campaign in order to find to have him brought before the Tribunal. They sought to accuse his direct involvement in the murders in order to get rid of the perpetrators following the incident.

The citizens in Paris were worried. Although violence was common during the revolutionary period however, it was currently on an upward trend. This was not simply isolated instances of people being killed due to their affiliation with the elite and uprisings throughout the nation and more brutal acts. Some who had thought in the beginning that bloodshed like this was to be expected, and even tragic was concerned about the increasing number of deaths and found it increasingly difficult to defend them.

In 1792, the election for a next National Convention took place. Robespierre was able to get anyone with a royalist leaning history excluded from voting or even from running. Then he was again enjoying a resurgence in his popularity. He was elected the first deputy to the National Convention, people seeing his previously scolded opinions on the conflict as shrewd and predictive.

Yet, just a couple of months after, attitudes changed. An enthralling military victory earned the support of military organizations and caused many to accuse Robespierre for the riots of September in addition to causing public opinions to shift towards the view the idea that the first attack on the Bastille was a crime. Robespierre was quick to respond in one his most passionate speeches "Citizens Did you really want an unconstitutional revolution? No revolution...We have to either accept or reject the riots completely. Making a criminal act of only a handful of apparent or true infractions that are inevitable amid an enormous upheaval could be a way to penalize those who had embraced the cause." Robespierre influenced the audience, and any further charges against him were put aside. Some of his most hated critics became more vocal.

In the month of December 1792 the Convention officially set Louis XVI on trial for Treason. The Convention ruled that he had committed treason. his Constitution of 1791, and certain people such as Robespierre considered the trial unneeded and demanded execution. He admitted that the he "abhorred" capital punishment but considered that "Louis must die because the homeland must live." Political enemies wanted nothing more than exile of the man. The discussion raged over the remainder of January, but on January 16, the issue was decided by an election. 387 of the members voted for of execution, and 334 of them voting against. Just a few days later, Louis XVI was executed. The king had died, the gap between traditional royalists and extremist republican groups would become unresolvable. France was open to threats of war and invasion by foreign adversaries for the sake of Louis.

Further financial issues soon arose because, while the prices of bread had remained stable but other commodities were been unable to do so. Many protested calling for fixed prices and Robespierre stood with their demands, however he was dissatisfied. Although he always seemed to support the needs of the people however, he was disappointed that the protesters were focused at things such as the price of soap. He began to suspect that there were more forces behind the tension, and that elites had been working with the masses in order to convert them to more base motives and then poison them to the growing Republic.

Chapter 14: Terror & Death

"Let the traitors die, so that the spirits of the murdered patriots are appeased, Marseilles is purified, liberty is avenged and strengthened against the blows of her cowardly foes!"

-Robespierre

In April 1793, Robespierre was of the opinion that death was required to punish "every attempt made against the security of the State, or the liberty, equality, unity, and indivisibility of the Republic." If they wanted to take out foreigners in the name of protecting the country, they should be prepared to execute the act in their own country, along with other residents, too.

The 25th March Convention under the direction of Robespierre established the Commission of Public Safety and an police force known as"the Committee of General Security. The civil war erupted between French forces from the west as well as

Parisian forces. The revolutionaries were able to convince supporters convincing the masses that the revolting French were sponsored and encouraged by Austrians. The war involved more than 1 million people both sides in the war, before the Spanish took over the Basque nation. Robespierre's foes, which is now named the Girondins were exiled by The Public Safety committee as he started to receive greater members.

In the following days, people began to clamor for the right to recall their deputies The Girondins - who, they believed, did not represent their needs anymore. After much debate and debate, the final decision was by the Convention could place these individuals under the guise of adversity to the interests of the country. Many fled, others were able to hide while a large number were held. On June 24 on, the Convention was able to pass a brand new

Constitution which was this time with far more radical republican ideas.

The nation was at turmoil. The Civil War consumed almost all of the resources for military, in a period of time where France was actually surrounded by growing enemies. This was accompanied by the English blockade that cut off the trade route and allies' connections to America. Eighty percent of government departments, in protest to the deportation and arrest of Girondins deputy ministers, were unable to accept the legitimacy that was the Convention. Robespierre created his rules that will determine his actions from now to the end: "A single will is vital. It has to be either republican as well as royalist." There is no room for grey areas that could be a compromise for Robespierre. Robespierre was appointed the head on the Committee for Health and Public Safety.

Robespierre thought that the sole actions to help save the Republic required censorship of oppositional works, the arrest of people who were hostile to the Republic and putting increasing resources towards the war effort. Robespierre was fighting, in his thoughts, a battle with two sides: internal as well as externally. The Committee was armed with more than ability to achieve these goals. They were able to issue warrants for arrest and choose individuals from various government or special committees, be accountable for the supervision of generals as well as other employees of the state and advising on foreign policy as well as control the budget of the secret services. Their only responsibility was not control was the police.

They began to implement the changes that radicals had pushed since the beginning of time. The feeling nobles were now facing the possibility of a "civil death." There was a price control, and the estates of nobles who fled was given to the peasants, and assistance was given to the most disadvantaged so that they could get the necessary. The new system of schooling had be created, since the majority of French teachers, who had typically been priests left, been detained or murdered. Robespierre supported a mandatory boarding schools, however the idea was never approved. The government planned massive celebrations and monuments to commemorate the splendor of the Republic.

It was not one instance when the federal administration made a decision on the policy which would later be referred to in the "Reign of Terror." Instead, it was a succession of increasing response, laws, and policy decisions taken in the face of ever-growing crises. Prior to the time that Robespierre was a member of to the Committee of Public Safety, the Revolutionary Tribunal sentenced fifty people to execution. The Tribunal was dismissed, and reconvened several times during the course of the Revolution and finally reuniting on March 10, 1793. In the final few months of its existence the Tribunal was awash with executions, and nearly 2100 people were executed, which included Marie Antoinette, Olympe de Gouges who was the king's cousin and the many others that had taken in the Tennis Court Oath at the start of the Revolution as well as an individual who Robespierre was friends prior to the outbreak that led to the revolution.

Robespierre was engaged in war. Robespierre was certain that they did not have distinct external and internal adversaries in the Republic however, he was convinced that any internal issues, not just one that was brought about by those who were part of the Revolution at its beginnings and were a result of international conspiracies. Refugees from other nations that he initially welcomed had now become infiltrators looking to destroy France. Every corner anyone could be found working in tandem with Austria as well as Prussia including high-ranking diplomats to fishermen. He was no longer dependent on the will of the populace, because the moment they spoke of a need contrary to the one he was able to believe that it was due to the fact that they were deceived.

A growing number of people were to be sentenced into the Revolutionary Tribunal on charges of conspiracies. The policy of many leading figures of the republic had changed to "there are no citizens in the Republic but the republicans." The further emboldening of the guillotining process boosted adversaries towards the Committee and they were able to present ever more often with sharper admonitions of their deeds. The resulting fear of paranoia only increased of a growing conspiracy in the minds of radicals. As of springtime it was reported that there were six thousand prisoners in Paris in the city alone.

One of the most terrifying instances was the case of Danton danton person who was Robespierre's close friend. Danton was a political figure which, at the time they were deemed royalist and criminal since he was among of the most conservative members and also faced allegations of corruption in the financial sector. There were charges brought against him. While Robespierre was initially reluctant however, he swiftly switched his position. The man was even criticized for his persona - that of a man who he wrote to saying, "I love you more than ever until death," in the wake of Danton's death. lost her life. The second major character who was to be raised, Desmoulins was a man whom the wedding of Robespierre was a guest at and was even playing in their child's play with them. The 5th day of April they were executed. There were laws which made it unlawful for anyone from outside the country to reside in Paris as well as anyone who was charged with treason could be investigated in Paris immediately.

Robespierre was granted the authority to select his members to the tribunal. In 1794's spring, Robespierre's as well as the power of his supporters was stronger and more centralized than before. They were able to crack down even more aggressively on their ever-stronger adversaries that could remain unaffected despite the ever-growing risk of death or incarceration.

Robespierre was tired. His years of suffering had taken an enormous impact on his health and he was forced frequently halt speechmaking and various other tasks to heal from several ailments. Although he was adamant about the executions of two friends from the past were essential to the benefit of the Republic but he was unable to be able to heal emotionally from the act or contribution he made to the execution. He was losing more confidence in the French population and was fighting for his life.

The assassination attempt began against his fellow radical leaders. The result was the last and most ferocious law that allowed for the possibility to detain those with the intention to "spread false news to divide or disturb the people," an extremely broad-ranging offense that could be used to justify nearly any thing. These and the tumultuous political controversies surrounding him and his own life, officially put an end to the friendship between him and his sibling, Charlotte who they shared a love of, and Charlotte was not able to stand by the choices that he or his Committee as well as the Tribunal made. Arrests and charges grew up to twenty-six per day in certain areas. The Tribunal could regularly decide and hear the cases of more than hundred people a day, some of them executed the following day in a manner ranging between forty and seventy people each day.

There are list of everyone that were executed during this period of time, together with the charges against them. A few of them include:

Henriette Frances de Marboef at the age of fifty-five, found guilty of waiting for the arrival Paris of Austrian as well as Prussian armies and stocking up on provisions for them. James Duchesne, Frances Loizelier, Melanie Cunosse, Mary Magdalena Virolle All of them convinced of writing. Genevieve Gouvon, aged seventy-seven and seamstress who was found guilty of a variety of conspiracies, since the start in the Revolution; Mary Angelica Plaisant the seamstress was executed for saying, "A fig to the country!.'

There has been some debate regarding the precise amount of power Robespierre held over the quantity of executions carried out during his time of five months, during the period during which he ruled his own Tribunal, Committee, and Convention. However, prior to his rise to power approximately four hundred persons were executed in the time of the Revolution. In the course of his five months in power, the figure jumped up into close to two and half thousand.

Though he never was an emperor who was ruled out of fear, he had numerous popular followers throughout his time, his seemingly endless and absurd charges, arrests and executions cost him a lot of his most loyal supporters. The creation of the Cult of the Supreme Being was supposedly intended to bring together both religious and non-religious revolutionary groups - caused concerns that he tried to establish himself as the god that was in doubt. The accusations of dictatorship were everywhere. His increasingly distant nature was due to emotional and physical illness was portrayed to as the rages of someone who resigned when he didn't get the way he wanted. The man was accused of conspiracy in order to assume the position which the king was unable to fill.

In August his arrest, along with several of his colleagues Tribunal members were detained at a gathering of the Convention and failed to convince the Convention they were not trying to overthrow the Revolution and take control of the situation by themselves. They took him into Luxembourg Prison, where the guards, who were commoners, were not keen to be detained for apprehension of one of the "incorruptible" man who held an almost popular cult in the majority of the United States. He escaped to the Town Hall with the other officers who were detained They quickly attempted to draft a paper that would establish the new Committee with a majority on the Convention:

Courage, patriots and Patriots of that Section des Piques! Liberty has triumphed! Already, those whose strength is considered to be a threat by traitors are now at liberty...the meeting will take place at Town Hall. Town Hall, where the courageous Hanriot is expected to carry out instructions from the Executive Committee that has been created to protect the nation.

The Convention was however, a group of troops and stormed Town Hall, at which the other deputy - Lebas had committed suicide using the help of a gun. Robespierre or attempted suicide or was killed at by soldiers while trying to write his name onto the affidavit.

In whatever way he sustained the wound, the shot struck his jaw and broke several teeth and then bleeding heavily. It was believed that he was dead at the time they found him, however they remained hopeful enough for him to be brought before a judge and sentenced to be executed along with others. The man was not able to talk due to the wound he suffered and they refused his masked requests for papers or pen.

After 17 hours of the shot and the arrest, Robespierre was the first out of 22 radical deputies who were to be executed. While en route to the spot there were chants from the crowd such as, "Is your majesty suffering?." After Robespierre ascended the scaffold and was executed, the executioner told the executioner, "There is a Supreme Being!," He ripped the face bandage apart and his jaw fell, his fingers dislodged. His final words weren't even words they were just a cry of pain that was agonizing.

Chapter 15: Representative Of The People

PLATE V

(Phot. Bibl. nat. Paris)

ROBESPIERRE was at Versailles to be a member of in the Third Estate of Artois just ahead of his 31st birthday. He, too, as thousands of his peers none of the political experiences, and most certainly not any experience in parliamentary politics. His reputation for being a powerful and knowledgeable lawyer, or a lawyer for the people and even a poor person's lawyer, was not widely known outside of Arras. The two pamphlets he wrote about politics did not reach beyond the region. France was inundated by pamphlets for over a year after the King removed the ban on censorship. Some are more significant and radical than the one Robespierre wrote: Abbe Sieyes had become famous after the publication of the book What Is the Third Estate? It wasn't just that Robespierre have no image, but his peaceful existence in Arras was not affected by his involvement in the highly-publicized national debates about reforms in which the Court was engaged in the last few days of the previous regime.1 There is little evidence that he took an involvement in these matters. However, even if he was just another provincial in the shadows at Versailles unnoticed by the countless others like him He had made public his opinions and announced his beliefs prior to leaving Arras. He was determined to fulfill his ideas as well as the self-image he'd declared.

The first meetings of the Estates-General, once the formalities of the opening of the sessions with a Te Deum in the Church of Saint Louis and a formal procession of the three orders of representatives--Clergy, Nobility, Commons--were held separately and were mostly taken up with administrative matters. Within the Commons the days were long of proving credentials, and the growing sense, expressed by many, that the three estates were, despite representing an overwhelming portion of the French population--Abbe Sieyes believed that to be the Third Estate composed 97 percent of the population--were not being given credit as well as there was a strong feeling that the three orders should be united to ensure that the nation would not be further divided in accordance with the old however artificial divides that had been that were inherited from the previous.

In the three weeks of the May 1789 in the third week of May 1789, Robespierre wrote to his Arras acquaintance Buissart an amazing letter to analyze individuals and politics and personalities, no new legislation was accomplished. The Commons were ensnared with internal disputes and had not yet declaring themselves as the National Assembly, they had not yet sworn that they would not break up until they gave France the constitution (as they did at the Tennis Court Oath of June 17) as well as they were not yet heard the plans of King. A "bourgeois revolution," as an historian describes the seizure of the idea by the Commons began barely in its entirety, and the great acts of courage were to come. The massive rural and urban turmoil of summer, which could have put the Revolution far beyond its dispersal through the armed Court did not take place. But Robespierre could see what other people did not see. A little over fifty years later this revealing letter was presented to the King Louis Philippe, who had been actively involved to the Revolution and was well-aware of the specific circumstances that were being examined: "It is perfectly exact," the King said.2 Robespierre's debut article as a researcher for the Revolution and showcases early in his professional career, his innate ability to do this kind of analysis. He doesn't pay attention to details and gets directly to the point of the matter: reform, not revolution is the main issue.

The clergy's power was swept away through the decree putting that ecclesiastical assets are available to the entire nation. The parlements, which were considered to be as a bastion for the aristocracywere given the next day the assurance of destruction. . . . The feudal aristocracy has been nearly eliminated. Most of the worst abuses appear to be gone with the help of people who represent the nation. Can we finally get our freedom? Yes, I think I'm able to ask this question.

The question was one Robespierre was likely to ask throughout the following five years. One of the characteristics of a fervent and shrewd mind which earned him respect and led to his followers' conviction that the Revolution was to be fought until its end. This He believed in the complete elimination of the counterrevolution and in all its varieties. Since the beginning of the Estates-General, this principle of faith was one of the principles he embraced. After the Revolution was started and fought, the Revolution had to be waged until the end. It was not a matter of compromise or expediency. of the equation. Sooner or later, they'd be viewed by him as yet another type of the counterrevolution.

In June, the Commons had their first victories in the revolution and could oust the estates-general with their three orders and establish themselves as one legislative body in the near future to be referred to as the Constituent Assembly, the bourgeois revolution, which was largely legally and judicially oriented began its initial step. The victory over the Bastille in Paris (July 14) was to consolidate the first victory and even bring Paris into the hands the Revolution. Massive riots across the countryside that took place in late summer known as the Great Fear, would not just expose the underlying flaws of the crumbling regime, and its failure to properly police its nation and even to reform it however, they would trigger the night of dramatic violence on August 4, as nobles voluntarily disposed their feudal privileges as well as the demise of the feudal era of restrictions on property and the people. In the early autumn, in the fall, the Constituent Assembly ruled. The dismantling of churches and the proscription by law of nobility, legal limitations on the King's authority as well as the creation of the first French constitution had to be completed. The first few days of the revolution had transformed France into a nation of parliaments. The whole nation considered the Constituent as a source of revival.

Robespierre was a participant in the parliamentary battles as well as in Jacques-Louis David's incomplete painting of his participation in the Tennis Court Oath he was recognized as a major figure in the ranks of oath-takers. Although he may have partially made his way out of the shadows of obscureness, his political philosophy of of morality and even of messianic convictions, were not met with many supporters. The constituent was an place of opposition and was a stumbling block for Robespierre. Most of his suggestions were rejected by Deputies. Some of his more reformist ideas were viewed as threateningly radical. Robespierre defended positions which had very little support within the Constituent however, the principles of democracy (one man one vote) as well as the removal of privileges that had remained since the old regime are important to any democratic society however, they were not radical in the least but he was resisted and ignored. A major reason for this apart from being concerned that process of democratizing France was a mistake and could cause some form government by mobs and a restraining order, was the manner in which Robespierre went challenging his fellow colleagues. Robespierre was always supportive of his ideas and also gave his auditors (even without being required) with moral opinions as well as moral interpretations of the Revolution. They did not need advice from him. They saw regeneration as removal of the obvious and vile corruptions that were a part of the old regime. This was achieved with as little disturbance as is possible. This would bring health back to the entire nation. Robespierre was even more frank. Moral stridency in his life was viewed with a righteous smirk as a warning to anyone who was against his views. Additionally, his insistence upon the goals of the Revolution as well as its aides led him to be seen as a magnanimous.

Through regeneration Robespierre saw not just the world that was cleansed of implacableness, resentment and insularity; rather, he imagined a new world by a community of individuals who had been recommitted to the general good. The man regarded fundamental revolution as morally important. The goal that was the goal of Revolution Revolution was to alter our nature as a whole. The motivation for this was found in the famous line from Rousseau's Contrat social: "he who is willing to build an entire nation should view himself as being involved, so to think of it, in changing the humanity's nature."3 Robespierre did not have any hesitations in committing to such endeavor.

The Constituent, just like the rest of the assembly of the Revolution were bourgeois in the social structure, and comprised predominantly of lawyers. About half of its members were, just like Robespierre Provincial lawyers. This type of professional training could resulted in a sense of caution and a lot of respect for rules along with a preference of judicially-based distinctions. In addition, many of his colleagues believed that he was to be too bold when it came to his suggestions. Collectively, they were the more openness to negotiate and compromise; they saw politics as a sequence of decisions that could be in line with the principles but also accommodating to the needs of circumstance and personality. They had absolutely no wish to change the human condition And certainly many believed that this was beyond their reach. They did not in principle have a problem with legal equality or to various freedoms of speech and press, in press and speech as well as gathering and worship. However, all of these rights must be realised and implemented within the environment of corporate and self interests, customs and convenience. The definition of freedom must be carefully crafted and careful protection against licenses, as well as careful limits and qualifications imposed by law. The moral imperative of Robespierre that pierced through all of this and was in danger. In the wake of it, as the Constituent believed it was a cause for disorder and an incitement to social unrest. Robespierre was not able to, either during the Constituent as well as in the Convention that was later his seat demand an attack on the property of others, an elimination of social divisions or an overall social equality, even though his name was often attributed to advocating for such things. However, the people who he called for at the start of his life was not part of the assembly. The cult of his followers was one of the main reasons that he was distrusted by his peers. The idea of bending the procedure of the Constituent and taking the streets in a way to establish the foundation of power in politics and power was a crime.

This was a rumor that was exaggerated. Robespierre did not go as far towards the

Left like his adversaries claimed that they believed he was to be a radical who was slightly more unsavory than Marat can be instructive. Robespierre did not get the chance to be referred to by his fellow members, whether during the Constituent or at the Convention in any authoritative position available up to the summer of 1793. Robespierre was averse to the majority of the Constituent due to his radicalism and would become so later however, in the following time, he as well as the Revolution were on the left. Another of the astonishing consistency in his life.

In the Constituent, he repeatedly appeared on the podium to make a proposal and also to voice his displeasure. His first speech was made on the 18th of May (almost two weeks before the meeting started) in which he made a statement regarding the clergy (VI 251). The first eight weeks of the Revolution Robespierre was at the tribune, or the speaker's dias was known at least twenty-five times. In 1790, Robespierre was present at the tribune for more than 80 times, and between November 1791 to the end of September 1791, he was there more than 60 times. At the start, those who felt his politics as well as his character unattractive were loud. They accused him of speaking excessively about himself. The accusation was of intransigence. It was alleged that he exhibited the pomposity of his appearance and that portrayed moral superiority. He was also accused of the arrogance of his opinions and their outrageousness, which he kept. This list of grievances from the beginning that contained only a few additional items, most notably an apparent hatred of dictatorship - - would often be used against the man. The catalog of insults and flaws is just as telling about its subject as the people who wrote it. This is a listing of what he was afraid to do, but not necessarily a realistic representation of what his peers were afraid of about him. One of the most striking aspects of the revolutionary Robespierre's career that is, a career in parliamentary politics one of the reasons he failed to be rather unsuccessful as a politician or as a leader. When he was a leader or politician in the Constituent just one of his legislative suggestions were accepted, and during the Convention, he was only in two of the assemblies, he wasn't a force of the debates or arguments and could not manage to overcome the resistance towards his ideas and personality through the control of a close organisation in the parliamentary system that could generate majority votes. In fact, he was the exact opposite.

What power Robespierre held to the Constituent and in the Convention which he incorporated into sessions outside of its boundaries. His popularity was beyond the boundaries of the National Assembly, Robespierre's colleagues were both feared and hated. This led to a sense of disdain and suspicion of the politician who seemed to be representing an enormous, possibly riotous unrecognizable segment of the population. The man was not, as the majority of his opponents who were members who was a member of the Assembly that was completely dependent on the Assembly, completely committed to its needs and rights. The president was not elected He never even sat at the table of secretaries but he was not a member of or commanded any major (or not so important) committee. It was only in the gloomy summer of 1793did he make the decision to head a committee, with conflict raging across the western part of the nation, with Lyons the second city within France that was in full protest, along with the Southeast similarly agitated, when the war with foreign powers was stalling and large areas of the country beyond the control of the federal government and only after four years of revolutionary turmoil in the summer of 1793, on the 27th day of July the members of his group chose for him to be a member of the Committee of Public Safety. This decision was a shrewd decision as it was made following the purge of the Convention and a couple of months after the famous Committee was first formed. Robespierre was forced to wait quite a long time to gain his power. The only authority he gained, and the sole power that the Revolution would allow it, was collegial. He was a part of the committee's governing the Revolution together with his eleven fellow members.

The fact that this wildly popular person was in such a position of his position of power is an interesting fact. Whatever reservations you may have about his political or personal life the fact is that he was hated. His false claim of his aspirations to the regime is clear evidence. In addition, he was distrusted by a majority of his colleagues in the deputy position in the beginning as well as at the conclusion of his tenure. It's important to keep in mind that the vast majority of those members of the House were backbenchers. They did not take an active or prominent part in discussions or debates. They were not able to draw attention to themselves which led the criminal Carrier to claim that they were only known to their people who paid the. The backbenchers who were when they were in the middle of the revolution, were able to be dragged from the shadows-- as were they at times during the agonizing rolls-call elections of the Revolution. However, as a whole, they sought peace rather than war and felt at home with the leaders of parliament who did not just cater to their needs, but also offered an easy and safe choice. They were known, with a snarky smile in the context of the Marais as the water that surrounded those on the left and right. The Marais have the majority on voting between opposing factions, it also held an overwhelming majority in those in the National Assembly. Parliamentary business couldn't be accomplished without their hesitant votes. Robespierre along with others, made his argument towards the Marais however the Marais was unduly strict when it came to his dealings with them. He more often than not created an impression of being focused more on impressing people that were outside of the Assembly--the Paris radicals, or Jacobins and Jacobins both Parisian as well as provincial -- than getting the deputies who were not committed. Robespierre was not an easy charmer.

Throughout his entire career, the Marais did not listen to his pleas or arguments and arguments, but also antagonistic. They were unable to agree to an oath with any of the left or right in a show of pity Robespierre was averse to, and weren't planning to throw their weight into the political machinations Robespierre believed in. It's difficult to convince the people one dislikes. Moral imperatives of his as well as his self-depictions as being more valuable than other people as well as his risky plans to increase democratic government and his concern for those in need and the poor, as well as his unsavory acceptance in Paris streets, usually from the most hated militants, drove the Marais to explore other avenues. His name was often associated with Marat as his critics were shrewd enough to predict that this would increase suspicion towards Robespierre as well. The two men created social phobias within the Marais as well as all over the Constituent.

Although many of those who were loyal to his policies that followed the uniformed line of robespierriste There were others who did it reluctantly. Within the middle of Jacobins Jacobins those who were not officially able to set the policy but had been trusted to carry out various tasks beyond Paris due to their leadership credibility and determination, there were reservations regarding Robespierre. They were the core of the Jacobins and, once they were finally banned and exiled, they accepted what was happening with no intention of abdicating their convictions. After the humiliation of defeat, some cited their loyalty to Robespierre who they felt little affection. Rene Levasseur and Jean Dyzez just to mention two robespierristes with a reluctance to wear who claimed they were loyal to Robespierre because he was the sole acceptable option and the sole ideology that lead to the major objectives of liberty, equality and fraternity to whom they first been a part of the Revolution. Robespierre did not enjoy the respect of his followers since he wasn't loved by anyone. As his supporters overcome their doubts, even the Marais was eventually able to conquer its anxieties. After Robespierre finally was appointed to the top position at the convention--and he had did not exercise an exclusive personal authority, even at the peak of his career --his power had grown indispensable and irresistible.

In the beginning of his professional career, persistence was the most prominent quality. The tribune was frequently belittled by the awe-inspiring crowds arranged by his foes. He was not deterred and was determined to continue his climb up the tribune. He soon became an advocate on behalf of the Artois deputation both by his fellow artisans as well as the Constituent. The fame, even if it was accompanied by a paid personal, was beneficial. In June, the undiscovered provincial was able to be heard in some way, or there was a decrease in the level of noise which greeted all speakers as a witness was sent to his journalist in Arras.4 Although his opinions were also shared by only a few of his coworkers He gradually began to be considered not in the sense of being eccentric or crank, but rather as an individual with something worth saying. A sign of his growing standing, even though there's any dramatic conflict, or a one awe-inspiring speech that we could refer to as the pivotal moment, is the place slowly given to his talks in newspapers. Newspapers start to write about their speeches with precision and accuracy and even pronounce his obscure name.5

Robespierre addressed virtually every issue that was raised prior to the Constitution, though Robespierre didn't have much to speak about issues of administration or economics. He was particularly concerned about issues of equality in society along with political democracy as well as the Constitution. The issues would continue to draw his attention. Through the entire Constituent, he threw his weight behind and agreed with laissez-faire laws supported by the majority of his votes and also endorsed the huge expropriations of property belonging to the church by the tangled legislation known by the Civil Constitution of the Clergy (1790) which was one of the main pieces of legislation that revolutionized the world. It took away the church's global wealth, while exposing its clergy to discipline by the state. "The clergy," Robespierre asserts (here completely in agreement to the majority), "is not a landlord. It is not right for religion as well as for the state or for the state to become a landlord."6 The fact that he was willing to see the church evicted and controlled by the state didn't reduce his concerns for those with holy orders who were permanently interrupted. The bishop made a plea to "the humanity of the Assembly" to ensure the protection of "old ecclesiastics" who had the only "poverty and their infirmities" in order to demonstrate their lifetime of dedication and commitment (VI 437). He was averse to privilege, as clear in his criticism of the generous benefits given to bishops who were forced to retire because they were not willing to join the Revolution and the less privileged clergy did not receive the same importance (VI 408). However, when the biggest law governing the legal rights and obligations of the labor and businesses, the Le Chapelier law was voted on and passed, Robespierre stood silent. The law allowed all labor groups and combinations of workers as in the case of manufacturing companies however this was not as than socially dangerous--to be banned. The defenders of the sans-culottes could not believe that their interests were better served by their personal groups. The assumption that the needs of all those in the lower classes, or those in the middle class, should most effectively be met by general-based revolutionaries instead of movement groups, which influenced the stance of Robespierre. It was not his intention to be like some have claimed, averse to economic concerns. He believed that they were less important as ideololgy (as was virtually every other person in the moment). He was also not hostile towards workers. He was a member who was a bourgeoisie man incapable to compromise on questions of class, as was also the case. He was adamantly opposed to any organization which could create an atmosphere of unity. special interests that could be in interfere with the overall desire. He believed that the best interests of the masses could be served best with the success of the Revolution and the Constituent. This was during the Constituent was the result of his democratic ideas as well as the reversal of existing privileges while preventing any new ones from arising. In these matters, he was a voice that was largely unheard, with no followers or factions, and was frequently accompanied by his friend, Jerome Petion. The majority, however, was in favor of the type of democratic egalitarian system Robespierre was a proponent of and was able to articulate.

France could be revived, Robespierre believed, through the use of good law. In the creation of a democratic society based on the principle of equality between men and women that was guaranteed by a constitution was vital. The legal power of a nation could be utilized in order to achieve liberty by means of force when necessary. In the footsteps of Rousseau who saw the law to be a means of social transformation and was just as the same as his teacher in his determination to force people to follow what they believed was right. In the area of freedom of speech as he viewed them to be not as important as the use of law in order to improve the country, he held good liberal ideas. He advocated for the freedom of expression (VII 140) and freedom of press (VII 321) and freedom from arbitrarily searches (VII, 541) as well as freedom from the censorship (VII 459) as well as the freedom to protect personal correspondence (VII 85). He argued that judges should were chosen (VII 26, 26) and demanded jury members elected by citizens (VII 65) and equally punished for all crimes committed by the armed forces (VI 507). He shared the belief of his generation in the necessity of constitutional reform, but he strongly opposed the success of the attempt to exempt large numbers of the citizens from enjoying the full rights of citizens, rendering the poor "passive and unimportant citizens of a public body."7 He advocated for regular elections (VI, 778) and a democratic approach to the militia of the future as well as in particular, the National Guard (VI, 622)--both of which he was unable to obtain--an unrestricted rights to request (VI. 451) and the most important legislative victory during the Constituent, the decision that deputies can not be elected (VII 408 819-20; VIII 419-20). His esprit de corps, which was a scourge among the labor and manufacturing groups he was equally afraid of in his coworkers. Deputies were paid to prevent their people would be handed "up to the aristocracy of the rich" (VII, 36) And he claimed in favor of "each deputy belongs to the people and not to his colleagues" (V, 161). The deputy himself was without source of income other than his pay, so he grudgingly returned a portion of his salary in Charlotte (X, 111).8 Much more radically, he sought that citizens be armed, as the best protection against intrusion by the state (VII 288) which it would continue to fight for.

In a variety of small issues, particularly those that dealt about the rights of small and marginalized people, he was interested. He considered prejudices towards performers "absurd" in itself and detrimental in a world in which the theater must be an integral part of "public schools of sound morals and patriotism" (VI, 160). Modernity and rabidness prompted him to insist that Jews were citizens as they were made the enemy of the oppressors. The purpose during the Revolution to end those "national crimes" committed against Jews as the sins that are that they are accused of being "our own injustices." If Jews are excluded from new society, it was based "on the violation of the eternal principles of justice and reason which are the basis of all human society." The same man was adamant about the slavery system and demanded that citizens be granted to the "men de color," which was the name used for non-whites in the colonies. The majority of them were white people, which, the spokesman argued is equivalent to asking an assembly "half composed of ecclesiastics and half of nobles" to decide whether they thought there was a need for the Third Estate ought to be considered (VII 349). "Let the colonies perish," said he instead of letting slavery endure (VII 362). Slaves weren't owners of property. "Ask this man who sells human flesh about what property is. He'll tell you with this long coffin he describes as the ship, inside which are chained and locked people who seem to be alive. rightful property. I purchased them for so the price in terms of dollars per person.' " "Ask this person who has land and ships" He continues in a provocative manner, "or who believes that the universe must be rearranged to allow him to acquire more property. He will offer you similar thoughts regarding the property" (IX, 466)). He wisely removed the offensive notion of the private ownership of slaves in the version that was published of the address. The slaves were never forgiven.

He was unsuccessfully opposed to every attempt to limit the scope of his franchise through imposing an obligation to own property. The Constituent was tied to tax collected, creating two types of people; "active" and "passive" were the terms used to describe that time. Robespierre's belief in the democratic system was founded upon the ability of the poor to protect themselves from the wealthy, as the goodwill of people was not always reliable (VI 131,). The government was obligated to guarantee universal participation.9 And Robespierre was passionate about a responsibility to safeguard "the weak from the strong" (V 18). Everyone who didn't achieve this had been "tyrants, oppressors, slaves, the national enemies of equality" (VII, 472).

As a result of the democratic tendencies, Robespierre wanted severe limitations of the King's authority. The King must only be the status of a magistrate. In his utmost concern for concordance of things and words and actions, he required for the King to "be called the first public functionary, the chief of the executive power, but never the representative of the nation" (VII 614). The Constitutional amendment that restricted the king's position exclusively to the Bourbon family and provided many privileges that were not available to other citizens, created "a family distinct from the other citizens . . . It's absurd!" (VII, 664-65). It was also political risky, leaving during this Revolution "the indestructible root of the nobility" (VII, 669). The only way to give this insanity an veto on legislation it continues to argue and even an indefinite one that would only block legislation for two legislative sessions but not completely destroy them would be "to annihilate the first principles of the constitution" (VII, 612-

13).10 Leaving the King with a large constitutional authority but preserving some exclusive privileges--a unique type of legal immunity to all crimes, with possibility of withdrawing the oath he took under his constitution, leaving from the country or fighting against his citizens--merely put off the process of what Robespierre believed was the inevitable confrontation between the monarchy and the Revolution. He was the King. counterrevolutionary leader to Robespierre.

Printed in the USA
CPSIA information can be obtained
at www.ICGtesting.com
LVHW010730161023
761195LV00003B/108

9 781777 597641